C0-AXE-721

The Lorette Wilmot Library
Nazareth College of Rochester

LIVING
IN THE
MIDDLE

LIVING IN THE MIDDLE

SHERPAS OF THE MID-RANGE HIMALAYAS

DONNA M. SHERPA

WAVELAND
PRESS, INC.

Prospect Heights, Illinois

DISCARDED

LORETTE WILMOT LIBRARY
NAZARETH COLLEGE

For information about this book, write or call:
Waveland Press, Inc.
P.O. Box 400
Prospect Heights, Illinois 60070
(708) 634-0081

Copyright © 1994 by Waveland Press, Inc.

ISBN 0-88133-745-5

All rights reserved. No part of this book may be reproduced, stored in a retrieval system, or transmitted in any form or by any means without permission in writing from the publisher.

Printed in the United States of America

7 6 5 4 3 2 1

915.496
She

To
my darling Phurba,
whose brain I have picked ruthlessly,
and
to the people of Bhuwa/Shurkey,
who have adopted me as one of their own

If God had not created the Sherpa, Everest might yet be unclimbed . . . like a strong mountain goat, humble, sturdy and swift, he climbs carrying loads up the precipitous and treacherous ice, rock and snow slopes, through inclement weather, biting winds and many other serious mountain hazards until the loader of the expedition prevents him. The fantastic endurance and equanimity of the Sherpa, his friendship that never fails, company that always cheers, his assurance born of skill and courage have few parallels in mountaineering history. He is the true Tiger of the Snows and without him so much by so many could not have been achieved, certainly not at such little cost in money and life (Sarin and Sing 1981).

Table of Contents

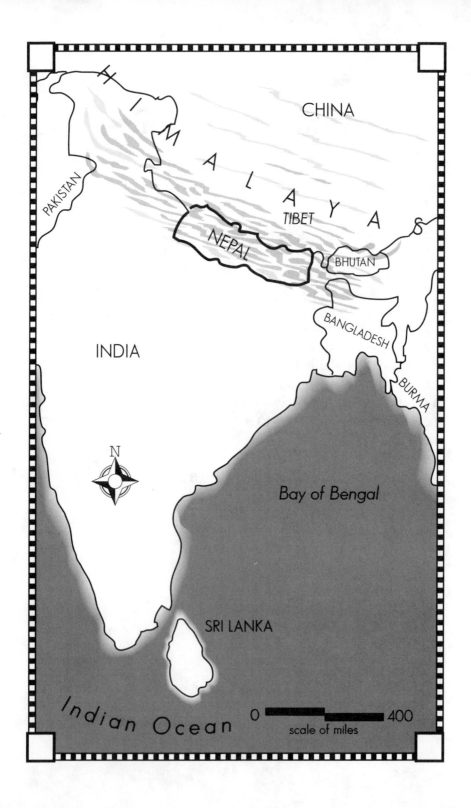

Introduction

This is not a doctoral thesis. Therefore, I could, but I need not, bore you with complicated quotes, sources, native phrases, and the like. I have found through my study that although the Sherpa are an ethnic group, they vary greatly from village to village. So if I were to reel off complex native phrases, and just say you learned them and went to Nepal, you probably could not find the region in which to use them. From time to time I have mentioned such things when they seem most appropriate. What I have tried to write is a cultural-anthropological study of the Sherpas. I feel that a work of this sort is essential. The Sherpas are rapidly turning toward the modern world. Their language is unwritten so all knowledge is passed on by word of mouth. If special care is not taken to record their story, I fear it will quickly be forgotten.

I received a Bachelor of Science degree in secondary education and history and have taught social studies at the secondary level for sixteen years. Of those years I spent ten years teaching cultural anthropology. Then I traveled to the Himalayas. I have always been fascinated with the Tibetans so naturally I was interested in the Sherpas with their origins in Tibet. On my fifth trek on the trails of Nepal I met and married a Sherpa. He is from the village of Bhuwa/Shurkey in the Everest valley.

I have not endeavored to describe Sherpa life in all regions and villages. It is impossible. Therefore, I have centered my story around Bhuwa/Shurkey, a village of about seventy adults, one hour's walk south of Lukla in the Khumbu District. There life is lived on a very basic level. I have spent some time in Bhuwa/Shurkey, but more importantly my husband, Phurba, spent the first twenty-four years of his life there. Through him, and research, I have gathered the details herein.

One problem with village names is that the Nepalese have one name which is listed on maps but the Sherpas sometimes have a Sherpa name for the same village. I will refer to the villages as the Sherpas do and after a slash include the Nepalese name.

Try to put yourself into these pages. Imagine what it would have been like if you had been born in the Himalayas. It sounds romantic at first, the mountains, the fresh air, the adventure, but like everywhere else there is no perfect place. Life there is like life anywhere—gratifying, frustrating, joyous, difficult. In the pages that follow, I try to bring alive contemporary life in one Sherpa village.

1

Getting There
Land and People

I hear the stirrings of cattle and people. Tiny bells begin to tinkle far off as gray light filters between the wooden shutters. When I disentangle myself from my sleeping bag, I push the shutters open to let out some of the suffocating smoke. The first rays of the sun are illuminating the tops of the mountains a soft pink. As I watch, the color slowly changes to orange and eventually all color seeps away. Temba is bringing wood upstairs; Mama is off behind the house; Lhakpa lets the cows and chickens out; Mingma is stirring the fire for morning tea; Dawa is rolling up the foam mats and stacking blankets on the shelves. Mama arrives and suggests rather loudly that Phurba get up. Another morning. Another adventure in the Himalayas, of trying to find out who I have become.

Exactly halfway around the world from the United States on the India subcontinent is the little-known kingdom of Nepal. Most people realize vaguely about where you are talking when you mention the Himalayas. Born just some sixty million years ago, they are the youngest and tallest mountains in the world. They rose from the sea floor, pushed back the water and established a new land world. They also changed the world around them by blocking the monsoon winds from the south and turning the lush green lands to the north into dry grasslands.

Surely the change took so long that the life forms of the area knew not what was going on. Some animals merely had to migrate to find better climates, while others, along with much plant life, died out. This was not a small happening in the world. The mountains continue to be a major influence today. The indigenous people, animals and plants are all sculpted and molded by the mountains.

We can find people half the world away who have never set foot in the Himalayas, yet they are also greatly influenced by them. Mystery, romance, fear and a myriad of other emotions are engendered in thinking about and studying about these mountains.

Just imagine Mount Everest—29,028 unbelievable feet above sea level, the tallest mountain in the world and probably the most spellbinding sight that one could hope to see. Thousands have struggled endless days and endured substantial pain just to cast their eyes upon it. Others have given up great parts of themselves to set foot on it and wrestle with the giant for its peak. It is almost a religious cause. Climbers have reached so high that they felt they could commune with the celestial spirits. They had done what many would like to do and others wonder about.

Some take a try at the third tallest mountain, Kanchenjunga, at 28,208 feet; or the fourth, Lhotse, at 27,923 feet; or the fifth, Makalu, at 27,824 feet; or the sixth, Dhaulagiri, at 26,810 feet; or the eighth, Annapurna South, at 26,504 feet or . . . Most of the world's tallest mountains are all together in this tiny country the size of Arkansas.

About 19 million people live in Nepal. The capital of Kathmandu has a population of 422,000 but the people are rapidly outgrowing the city limits (World Almanac 1990).

Himalaya in Sanskrit means "Home of Snow" or "Abode of Snow," if you are more poetic. The Nepalese call Everest *Sagarmatha* and to the Tibetan it is *Chomolungama*, "Goddess Mother of the World." It does seem a bit trite to refer to this great slab of rock by the name of a British map maker who never seemed to have set foot near the mountain. According to Malla, "The Himalayas are built of a thick sequence of mesozoic sediments. Only a few small deposits of mica, zinc and iron have been found in this zone so far" (Bhatta 1977). At present, I am not nearly as concerned with what is under the surface as to what is living on the surface.

The mountains have helped to make the people what they are. Westerners are fascinated by those who live in the high altitudes, the Sherpa. About 35,000 Sherpa are believed to live in Nepal today (Kunwar 1989). They have several centers of habitation scattered across the country, but the most famous is the Solu Khumbu Valley, the valley of Everest. The valley is divided into two sections: the Solu and the Khumbu, with the long Pharak Valley connecting the two. They remind me of a set of weights. As you will see there are many interconnections between the Solu and Khumbu. Those who live there do not consider the two regions as one, since they are so different in peoples and climate. Many different ethnic groups of people live in the lowland Solu: Tamangs, Thamis, Brahmins, Kshatriyas, Jirels, Newars, Magars, Rais, Gurungs and Sherpas.

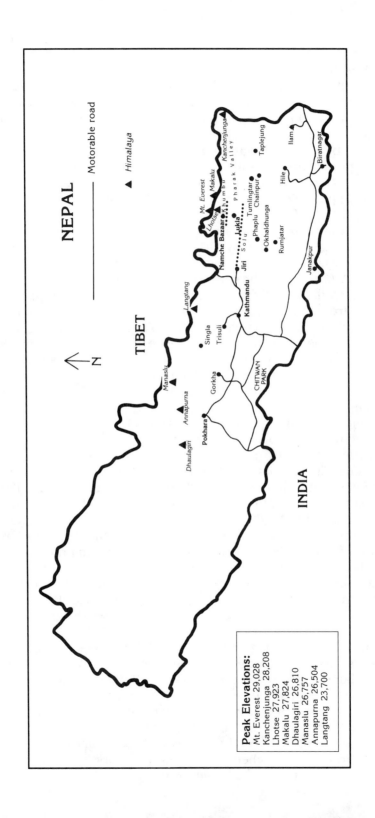

The Khumbu is predominately Sherpas. North of Nauche/Namche Bazaar, Tibetans who have arrived in the last hundred years are called Pepba. My husband's village of Bhuwa/Shurkey is in the Pharak Valley. One hour south of the airport at Lukla, its altitude is a mere 7,700 feet.

It can be assumed that the Sherpas originated in Tibet, since the Sherpa are Oriental and speak Sherpa, a relative to the Tibetan language. The other ethnic groups of Nepal have their origins in India and speak Nepalese, the official language that is a cousin to Hindi.

Five to six hundred years ago the first Sherpas came to the Khumbu. Whether driven by hunger, territorial disputes, religious strife, or invasion (Mongols), they descended from the high Tibetan plateau (12,000 feet) to the various elevations of the Khumbu. Since Sherpa means "Man from the East," we can assume that is the direction from which they came, usually thought to be the land of Kham a relatively flat plateau in Tibet. They stayed together after arrival because of their vast difference from the other peoples inhabiting the country. The whole nation of Nepal seems to be this way. Though there is some intermarriage, considering how long the Sherpa have been in the nation it is amazing how ethnically pure they are. For hundreds of years after their arrival, the Sherpa maintained active trade with their native land of Tibet. Communism closed off trade and isolated Tibet in 1959, but gradually some small bits of trade have begun.

Frequently, authors have referred to the Sherpas as the "Tigers of the Snow." It is quaint but hardly tells much about them. They are a people who had to change their entire way of life from herd tending on the flat lands of Tibet to farming in the mountains of the Khumbu. It must have been a struggle in the beginning. We can only surmise, since no one could write anything down. Even today the Sherpa language is a nonwritten one. In this uphill and cold land life is hard, yet the people seem ever smiling, joking and giggling uncontrollably. Bringing two Sherpas together rarely results in a serious conversation; teasing is always the order of the day.

It is difficult to imagine a society without wheels, since they are things we take for granted everyday of our lives. Wheels on cars, trucks, planes, carts, wheelbarrows—everything that decreases our manual labor seems to have wheels. The only common wheels in the Khumbu are prayer wheels. There are no roads in these mountains, only trails that are never flat. There is very little flat land, so anything with a wheel is worthless. It takes more work pressure to move the wheel than to do the work by hand.

It is not easy to get to Bhuwa/Shurkey from Kathmandu. If it is not the monsoon, flying to Lukla is possible on a twin-engine Otter plane. With only seventeen seats, one is unlikely to get a seat on the first flight of the day; chances are better for a ticket on the second or third flight of the day. Often the mornings in the Kathmandu Valley (4,400 feet) are foggy. The tiny planes fly by sight so they must wait for the fog to lift. Down drafts begin about noon and are another consideration. If the plane does not get off the ground by about eleven o'clock in the morning, it is not going that day. It could not possibly fight the winds to rise to Lukla at 9,300 feet. (Lukla is the Nepalese word for the airport town of the Khumbu; it means sheep.) Often the first flight takes off but the second and third do not, so some prefer to take a later date and get a first flight. In that way, a day is freed to look around Kathmandu, that fascinating capital with a mixture of old and new, clean and not so clean, Western and Eastern, Hindu and Buddhist.

Having secured a first-flight seat, there is great exhilaration— or perhaps stomach churning—while tumbling through the wind currents on the climb to Lukla, watching the terracing of the lower valleys recede and charting the roads that turn into tiny switchback trails. Then, it seems, out of nowhere a shelf in the mountains appears and the plane is crawling up toward it. Lukla literally takes your breath away. The plane ever so lightly touches down on the former cow pasture and bumps among the rocks as it rapidly takes you straight into a sheer cliff. You can feel the pilot fighting desperately to apply all the brakes he can; the plane vibrates and you know it will surely shake every rivet out. Your knuckles are clenched onto the seat arms and you swallow hard. At the last possible moment the plane makes a ninety degree right turn into a tiny field adjoining the Lukla "terminal." Most travelers descend the steps with very mixed feelings and wobbly knees. Can one really kiss the earth in a country not their own?

Never mind, grab your gear and a porter, if you can find one, and set out for Bhuwa/Shurkey. An hour south by the trail, there is a tiny plateau sticking out into a deep river valley, containing the entire village of Bhuwa/Shurkey. The Dudh Kosi (Milk River) flows far, far below. The river is named this because of the glacial silt it carries with it. The Dudh Kosi is also made up of the Bhote Kosi (Tibetan River); the two rivers meet many miles north beneath Nauche/Namche Bazaar, the so-called Sherpa capital.

If my husband and I happen to be flying with you, we would have to delay our arrival at Bhuwa/Shurkey, for we never leave Lukla for Bhuwa/Shurkey without meeting at least two relatives and having to go to their respective houses for libations. Word spreads fast in these mountains and, while at one relative's house, another often arrives to invite us over to their place. Of course, we

Lukla, the major airport of the Khumbu region. Though the surface looks smooth, the ride is actually bumpy. A plane has just taken off. Many will disappear below the sheer drop at the end of the runway, being pulled down by air pressure. Lukla was a sleepy little village until Sir Edmund Hillary helped to build the airstrip to aid expedition access. Now Lukla is a bustling village with practically every building a store, tea shop or lodge. As many as two hundred trekkers have been stranded here awaiting flights that had been cancelled due to poor weather. Shurkey is a one-hour walk south, to the left of the airstrip.

can not refuse. When we eventually arrive in Bhuwa/Shurkey much later that afternoon, we find that everyone knows we are coming. The grapevine is working again.

But what if it is the monsoon? Who would be foolish enough to go there in the rainy season when flights are impossible and footpaths are treacherous? If you are unlucky enough that all the flights have been canceled for days or weeks into the future or if you are a Sherpa without the means to buy a plane ticket, then you must take the bus. Even though a plane ticket for a Nepalese is about half the price that is charged to a foreigner, it is still too much for most people. The bus is about one-tenth the price of the plane.

For your money you get a spectacular view. The road, built with Swiss aid, is not in bad condition, unlike the road that goes west to Pokhara. The road east to Jiri, however, is only about one-and-

This is a view of Shurkey from one of the trekking lodges in the village. Mama's house is the fourth structure down the village on the right. The small shed with the rocks on the roof is a toilet; leaves are used as toilet paper and the contents are raked onto the fields immediately below the shed. This photo was taken in February, and already winter wheat is growing in the slightly darker field behind the center house. In the ravine to the left is a river. Between the village and the hill on the right is a drop of two thousand feet to the Dudh Kosi River.

a-third lanes wide. So, when two buses or trucks meet, one has to give way. With no guard rails and often thousand-foot drops, it can become quite thrilling, that is, if you are lucky enough to have an inside seat, and foreigners usually do. The roof gives better vistas but there is often not much to hang onto. Many people have catapulted off the tops to their deaths. From Jiri it is only a six-day walk to Bhuwa/Shurkey. For my husband it is only three days, but he has to slow down for me. We are working our way east over north-south ridges; it is constantly up and down. If it is raining violently, there is clutching mud; that is why so many natives go barefoot: it is easier to grip and therefore one is less likely to fall. As if the mud were not enough, there are also the leeches, those white threads that wiggle upward from every leaf awaiting your gorgeous blood-bloated arms or legs.

Along the way we stay the night in trekking lodges. They are set up in every village for the many people who hike Nepal without an organized trekking agency. Lodges tend either to have beds all together in one large room or to have individual rooms each containing two single beds. A bed with a cotton wadded mattress and blankets but no sheets or pillows can be purchased for about thirty cents a night if you also purchase meals or for about fifty cents a night without meals. Each lodge usually has a tiny shop to buy necessities, and hot meals can be purchased. Phurba always inspects the lodge to make sure that the roof is not leaking. We do not have any relatives in this area. If we did, we would stay with them.

Eventually, the Pharak Valley opens and finally at the extreme northern end is Bhuwa/Shurkey.

2

Getting Settled in
the Village

The Sherpa people are controlled by the weather, seasons, farms, trekking and money. Only 17 percent of Nepal is arable land, but 91 percent of the Nepalese people are engaged in agriculture. This brings the average Nepalese only U.S. $160 a year, a pitiful amount when compared to wages in the United States (World Almanac, 1992). Many villages in Nepal have remained ethnically pure. These are usually in isolated areas, but even in the accessible Kathmandu valley it is common to find ethnically pure villages, such as Newari villages with their distinctive row houses. Various groups have settled together, usually for economic gain, along major trade routes. Kathmandu and Pokhara, the largest cities of Nepal, are a jumble of all ethnic groups. Nonetheless, even in the cities the people try to settle into ethnic neighborhoods.

Rains of Life

Village life in the Khumbu revolves around the climate. The monsoon usually arrives in June and brings rains continuously until September. It is not that it rains twenty-four hours a day, but it is cloudy a great deal and rains at least once a day, sometimes very hard. Some days it rains all day. Most mornings are clear and afternoons are foggy. The Sherpas say that morning rainfall will make the rest of the day clear and that the foggy weather ripens the wheat. The monsoon swells the Shurkey Khola that flows through my husband's village. One advantage to this is that the water brings a lot of wood with it and the villagers gather what they

9

can before it is swept further down the river. The heavy rains after August are called Yerjyuk (end of monsoon); the last heavy rainfall is Tenjyuk, in September. It is said that the monsoon and fall are like two sisters fighting. It is the continual dampness that influences life so much. Farm work, travel, everything is done in the rain.

The temperature is usually in the seventies (degrees Fahrenheit), with the nights fairly cool. Temperatures, of course, vary greatly with altitude; the temperature at 12,000 feet and 7,000 feet at the same moment can vary as much as twenty degrees or more. It also depends on whether or not the sun is out. The air may be very chilly but, with the sun beating down through the thinned atmosphere of 8,000 feet, it can be very hot.

From October through March the villages are rain free. Crystal-clear days and nights in the high altitudes make me feel wonderful. The stars at night are so close I feel as though I can almost touch them. The Milky Way suddenly has millions of stars that I had never seen before.

The really cold months are December and January. The snows can begin in November and are usually gone by February. Two to four feet of snow per year is common in the Khumbu; however, on occasion, the yearly snowfall in the Khumbu will reach ten to fourteen feet. During these times, villagers living on the second floor of their houses can walk straight in a window from outside. Again, temperatures vary, but little melting takes place in these months. By February it is fifty degrees in the sun in the afternoon.

May can be especially warm and humid before the beginning of the monsoon and seventy-five degrees Fahrenheit can seem delightful, or even cool, when sitting under an umbrella reading a book. But when in the sun, breaking your back in the garden, seventy-five degrees can be a really hot day with sweat dripping off your nose. May can also be a time of high winds. Our village sits exposed on a high plateau that falls dramatically to the Dudh Kosi River. The winds roar up the deep river valley and sweep over the village often blowing off roofs and scattering everything that is not nailed down. Flimsy bamboo shelters nearly explode with the impact. Winds just mean more work for the farmers to rebuild.

The combined yearly total of rain and snow in the Khumbu is between forty-five and sixty-five inches. A substantial amount. My native Pennsylvania gets only thirty inches and we think it rains all the time.

The Himalayas are located at twenty-seven degrees North latitude—that is a lot closer to the equator than the United States, which ranges between twenty-five degrees North and forty-five degrees North. The temperatures are not warmer and are often cooler than in the United States because of the altitude. One thing

the altitude does not affect is the sun's rising and setting. It varies
a little with the season. In summer we can expect the sun to rise
at about five in the morning and to set at about seven in the evening.
In the winter, it is about seven in the morning and five in the
afternoon. Without the long nights of summer that we enjoy here,
the work of the day must be done during the light. Mountains also
influence the amount of available light. In my husband's village the
sun lightens the sky but does not actually shine on the ground until
half past eight or half past nine in the morning, depending on the
season. Likewise, the afternoons are cut short when the sun dips
behind the mountains at about half past four or half past five in
the afternoon. This means that early morning and late afternoon
summer work in the fields will be cooler. In the winter the best time
to do something outside is in the middle of the day in order to get
the sun's rays.

Steps and Stones

Villages are placed where there is available flat land. However,
there is so little flat land in these mountains that often the houses
are on the hills leaving the fields on the flat. Some terracing has
been done, most commonly in long, deep steps. In our village each
step belongs to a different family. Stone walls separate the fields
and keep the soil where it belongs; as the people cleared the land
of rocks, they used them for the walls.

Khumjung, to the north is a beautiful village of these gradual
steps with their low stone walls. In Nauche/Namche Bazaar the
fields are flat in the middle with the houses built on the hills
surrounding them in sort of a bowl effect. Phortse, north of
Nauche/Namche Bazaar, appears to be flat from far down the trail
but the village is again long steps of land sloping ever downward.
Lukla is a sort of mixed up jumble of fields and houses wherever
they can be placed. There are no set patterns to the villages; the
geography has always been the determining factor.

Houses are also made of stones, as are the walls surrounding
steps. There are masons who build the houses. The family wanting
the house must supply the labor of cutting the necessary wood and
stone, and bringing it to the assigned place. The mason is paid to
build the house. A two-story house, called a *khangba tyangang* in
Sherpa, costs about one thousand American dollars at today's
exchange rates. A one-story house, *khangba sam* or *sabkhang*
(smallest), about half that.

Before the builders start, the village *lama* (priest) blesses the
house. The village lama is an ordinarily dressed man of the village

Terracing is a way of maximizing arable land and has been accomplished over hundreds of years in the Kathmandu Valley. The population of Nepal is multiplying so rapidly that extreme measures such as these have been taken to increase the food supply. Crops can be grown in this tropical climate year round. It is also here that massive landslides occur during the monsoon season.

who also farms. He knows simple ceremonies and does these for the village earning, in the process, the title of lama. It saves a lot of time for villages who have no monastery and it saves the villagers a lot of money, since they do not have to pay to bring a lama from outside the area. The family brings a bucket of *chang* (home brewed beer); the lama inserts a piece of straw and flicks drops of chang to the wind while intoning a prayer. This is called *circem chetup* and is to bring good luck to the building of the house and to keep away the evil spirits. The villagers present at the ceremony then drink the beer.

Now work can begin. The family is obliged to help with the step-and-fetch-it chores. To their advantage, they do not have to house or feed the workers, even though they might be from another village. In the Khumbu no mud or cement is used between the rocks. The masons fit the rocks together and, when the walls are complete, the family mixes *dumbba* (red clay and water) by treading on it with their feet. This dumbba is then smeared over

The first house on the left is Mama's house. The roof shingles are held down with stones, and various bamboo mats are propped up against the house. The stone wall separates her field from the neighbors. The elevated section in the middle of the picture is designated for various jobs such as drying potatoes. The middle house is owned by a man who was once the wealthiest man in the village until he was cheated out of his money.

the rocks on the outside to form a smooth surface and plug all the cracks and holes. Most families then *puck* (whitewash) the clay.

The wooden parts of the house are made primarily from pine. There are three different types of pine in the forests surrounding Bhuwa/Shurkey. Window frames, doors, posts for the roof, roof beams, roof planks and the planks for the floor of the second floor are made of hand-sawed pine planks. These planks are no less than two-inches thick. Since the planks are sawed with a crosscut saw, it is almost impossible to saw them less than two inches thick. Then they are planed smooth with a hand plane. Villagers like to use mahogany for the roof. Quite a lot of mahogany grows in the surrounding forests. The *nyuthi* (benches) and shelving inside the house can be made of pine, mahogany or poplar. Tables are usually birch.

In the surrounding forests there are lands owned by individual families. The family who owns the land is the only one who can cut the trees that are used for boards. The scrub wood can be cut by anyone, but the varieties that are used for boards are not cut young. This is one way that the village has controlled the use of the forest for over hundreds of years and made sure that there would be trees left to grow large enough for boards.

Roof shingles are more complicated in that they come from the Sagamartha National Park, 460 square miles of land just north of Bhuwa/Shurkey. Once again, those families that have always owned the land that is now inside the park can cut their own trees; on the other land, where the surrounding villagers have always gone to cut, such harvesting has been curtailed. The government has done this by making the people register at Lukla for a permit to cut. When the permit is approved, the villager must pay one rupee (two cents) for every board that is cut. The government official must go to the forest with the villager and stamp each tree that the villager wishes to cut. The government does not permit the cutting of rhododendron, mahogany or pine. Much of the wood that the villagers have used for roof shingles has been cut from this area. Now it is nearly impossible because it is so costly. The locals are very upset about this. When I asked my husband why they just did not go somewhere else, he remarked that everywhere else was too long a journey. As it is, the distance is so great (15 miles, but a difference of 1,700 feet in elevation) that most people can only bring one load of wood a day from this forest.

Red and white oak are not cut by the villagers, because it is their leaves that feed the cows when the corn stalks run out and there is no grass available in late winter/early spring.

Windows and door frames can be painted, if the family can afford it. Color abounds as the people seem to prefer bright blues, greens and reds. Usually each window is painted several different colors. The window is one color, the molding another and the frame yet another.

When the house is completed, the lama repeats the circem chetup ceremony for good luck for those who live in the house. Everyone who comes to the ceremony brings something like tea or chang for the family. Then they have a big party and dance the night away. Usually the whole village attends, as no Sherpa likes to miss a party.

Two-story houses are the most typical, and our house conforms to the usual pattern. The first floor is divided in half. One half is for the storage of food, such as potatoes and corn; the other side is the stable for the cows and chickens. There are no goats, sheep or pigs in our village.

The second floor is one big room. One side has windows with benches under them that are anywhere from six inches high to standard chair height. Mama's hearth is also on this side of the room. Sherpa fires are considered sacred. I had read that they have seats of honor next to the fire for the most important guest and I have seen these in other villages, but our village does not seem to follow this tradition. If, however, the lama enters the house, a place

This is the inside of Mama's house: Dawa, Phurba's brother, is ready to sweep the floor with a broom handmade from twigs, a job done at least three to four times a day. In front of the windowframe on the right-hand side are low benches covered with a foam-rubber pad; in front of these is a higher bench with tea cups and bowls on it. Drying racks hang above the fire in the middle of the floor. Mama's bed is in the back right-hand corner in front of the shelves holding dishes. The entrance to the stairs to the stable is in the left-hand corner, where you can see the good-luck pictures of the chicken, teapot and chorten *(a Buddhist monument).*

is made beside the fire for him, but it does not contain a special rug or cushion as I have seen in other places.

In the corner is Mama's box bed. Phurba's father is dead, so the two smallest boys, aged seven and nine, sleep in the bed with Mama. The older children have foam-rubber mats that they place on the floor and cover themselves with thick cotton blankets. These are stored on shelves during the day. Shelves are placed against one or all three of the remaining walls. Here are stored the dishes; the plates are usually metal but there are delicate china teacups and saucers, and glasses. Most families have cutlery, but they are rarely used, as most people eat with their fingers. Also on the shelves are the pots and pans. The wealth of the family is measured by the number of large copper containers they own. Food is kept on the shelves, too: grain (wheat, buckwheat and barley), flour, tea, sugar, salt. Families try to keep as much as possible in metal containers so that the mice cannot get into the food. Most people do not have excess clothing but, if they do, that too is found here on the shelves, along with trekking boots, ropes, parkas and anything else that the family might own.

In the old days families owned wooden barrels. Today, they use large plastic barrels (usually blue) that have been gotten from expeditions. These are lined up along one wall and contain grains and chang.

Few families have any modern kind of lighting. The richer families have kerosene lanterns that have been used in expeditions and left behind, but they have to be able to afford the fuel and mantles, if available. Candles are expensive and also are not common. Some people have jars of kerosene with wicks that smoke terribly. Most families use only the light of the fire and go to bed when they are tired of sitting in the dark. Flashlights could be obtained from trekking and expeditions, but few families can afford the batteries, which are of poor quality anyway. To get around at night, people usually light a handful of grain stalks. I have often walked through the village at night with no illumination but the stars and moon.

While expeditions leave behind exotic goods, which are sometimes recycled, it is the natural environment to which Sherpa people usually turn to supply their needs.

The Forest

The forest, or jungle, as my husband calls it, is a vital part of the village. It contains necessary wood for building (the village controls who cuts what, except for family-owned trees). The forest provides other needed products: wood for fuel, bamboo for making many household objects, charcoal and medicines.

Wood is used for cooking and to keep the houses warm. Pine is never cut for fuel, because the resin it contains makes sparks if burnt. Oak is the best for the fire, but there must be enough oak in the forest to supply leaves for the cows.

My mother-in-law has a simple ring of stones on the floor where a tiny fire is always burning. To keep the floor from burning, stones are put down first and then plastered over with clay. Sherpas do not let their fires go out as the neighbors would comment about it—I assume the sentiment also means that it would be bad luck. We tend to brush good and bad luck aside these days, but the Sherpa really believe in luck and do everything they can to gain good luck and avoid bad luck. Some of the other houses have fire boxes, plastered in mud, and a sort of chimney that takes most of the smoke away. My mother-in-law's house has nothing. The smoke just fills up the house and filters out the windows. At night the fire is banked and little smoke is produced. During the day, no matter the temperature, the windows must be opened to allow the smoke an exit. Mama coughs constantly; her lungs must be black. Yet no matter what I have tried, I cannot get her to change her fire. I would love to bring in a wood-burning stove from the United States, but she would not want it. It would certainly heat the house better in winter. The idea of producing methane from cow manure does not seem to have reached the village, as it has in many parts of Tibet and India. As so often happens, even if the idea is introduced, the people do not adopt it because it is different or some taboo gets in the way. The Sherpas would object to the need to stir the cow manure and perhaps pollute themselves with it.

Mama's windows have no glass in them; only a few of the villagers have glass. The cost of someone bringing the glass up the trail on his back makes glass a luxury few can ever afford.

Very few women go to the forest to do the work there. The women tend the fields while the men are away in the forest, cutting wood for fuel twice a year or harvesting other forest products. In spring and fall the men go the forests when the hard work on the farm is done. They cut as much wood as they think they will use in the next six months. One medium-sized tree will keep a house in firewood for about a month. They split and stack the wood to dry. Several weeks later all the available men and boys of the village go into the forest and haul the wood in great loads on their backs to the village. Each person reciprocates. The Sherpas think that if you have no pile of firewood outside your house then you will have no *yang* (luck).

One year Phurba went to the forest and cut the wood. Instead of stacking it neatly in piles he just left it laying about to dry. While the wood was drying a fire began lower down on the trail. It was caused by the people who live about two- or three-day's travel down the Pharak valley. These people use grass for their roofs, and they frequently burn off fields so that the grass will grow well the next year. That year the fire got out of control and burned the whole way up to where Phurba had cut his wood. When he returned to haul the wood down, it was all burned up. The fire had been so hot that it had even cracked the rocks.

One of the problems in this region is the increased burning of wood due to the tourists. Conservation-minded trekking companies now carry kerosene stoves and do not provide campfires for the tourists. Lodges in the villages, however, burn wood for food preparation and warmth. The area around Bhuwa/Shurkey has been suffering since the government introduced restrictions to avoid over cutting. My husband worries about what his family will do in the years to come. To the casual observer the whole area seems to be surrounded by dense forest, but, considering all that is involved in managing the wood, one comes to understand that it is in short supply. In some of the lowland areas I have seen deforestation at its worst, with massive landslides as the result. In some of the higher elevations, deforestation is an extreme problem, since it takes much longer for the trees to grow back. Sir Edmund Hillary (renowned for his mountain climbing and exploring expeditions as well as for his work in the development of Nepal) has started a replanting campaign for the upper Khumbu. Others have also helped with the reforestation.

Those who live in villages above the tree line must burn cow dung. Cow dung is a very good fuel, burning long and hot and it does not smell. However, someone has to collect it, usually young girls, and form it into patties to be set in the sun to dry. Obviously, if it is burnt, the manure cannot be used for fertilizer; however, the leaves from the bottom of the cow stalls can be used as an excellent fertilizer.

Nepal is one of the most rapidly growing countries in the world, with a population of 19 million (World Almanac 1992)—up from 14.5 million (World Almanac 1981) only ten years ago. As the population increases in these fragile upland areas, there will be more demand for such things as forest products and the clearing of land. Rapid population increase will thus also contribute to deforestation.

In our own family, Mama had seven children, two of whom are already dead. A family must have enough members to do the labor and to take care of the parents in their old age. There is no retirement or social security in these mountains, so there is pressure for large families to ensure that children survive to adulthood, to provide both work and a social-service net.

Other woods in the forest include *sal* (soft wood) and rhododendron, which are used for carving. Rhododendron does not split, so it is made into the mortar to grind *martze* (chilis). There is an abundance of rhododendrons in the mountains. In spring entire mountains are pink, red and white with their blooms. Children use straws of bamboo to suck out the nectar deep within the flower but they are careful to stay away from the pollen which is poisonous. Some rhododendrons grow to enormous heights and widths. We are used to rhododendron bushes in the United States, but in Nepal they are trees. Orchids can be often found clinging to the trees. There are hundreds of different varieties of orchids growing throughout these mountains—a botanist's delight. With moss hanging from their twining branches, the forest can become very creepy, and I always expect a troll, pixie or gremlin to jump out at me.

The forest is the home of many spirits. Adults are usually not scared of these spirits, and they seem to be able to do no harm to adults. Children under the age of nine are only allowed in the forest with adults. If they were to go by themselves, the spirits would scare them and perhaps make them sick.

Leaves are gathered in the forest and put down in the stable for bedding for the cows. This material is then gathered up once a year and put on the fields as compost. We have an *ungma* (a little shed with only a roof and very low bamboo walls) where the leaves are dried until they are used. Very few houses have extra sheds to them.

There are many uses for forest bamboo. I was surprised to find that bamboo grows at this high altitude; one always thinks of bamboo as a tropical plant. Then I remembered the pictures of the pandas of China eating bamboo as the snow falls. In Sherpa country bamboo is used to make trays and baskets. The trays are used in the house for a multitude of jobs. *Gurmu* (smaller trays) are placed above the fire on frames to dry martze and other foodstuffs. *Galu* (larger trays) are used to winnow grains. The *tsaou* (baskets) are used to carry everything. Visitors immediately see their use on the trails, as porters carry everything up and down the mountains in bamboo baskets. (A porter on a trek is called a *mountain porter*. A *hill porter* is the term used for those who carry goods to the villages.) The villagers use the baskets to carry whatever wherever. Wood is carried from the forest in the baskets. Unbelievable loads are hoisted onto men's and boys' backs and brought to the village. The basket is held in place by a tump line which is passed across the forehead. I have seen young men of about eighteen who have carried so many heavy loads that there is a permanent indentation in their foreheads. The bamboo must be very strong to sustain such a load. My husband told me of loads he has carried that have actually weighed more than his body weight. I have seen great loads of hay on women's backs, as well, which have bent them over double. In a land with no wheeled vehicles, everything must be carried in some fashion. These people have chosen to use their backs. It is easy to imagine the back trouble such loads must produce.

In the monsoon season, bamboo is used to shelter cows in a structure having only poles and a roof. Some families that do not have enough fodder for the cows gather grass in the forest and dry it for the winter. In January, February and March, when the corn stalks have all been used up, the boys go into the forest and cut

A Sherpa woman expresses the weight of the hay she is carrying in her basket, which is secured with only the strap (tump line) across her head. Similar loads are carried daily up and down the trails of the Khumbu region—everything from food to lumber.

oak leaves (new green leaves have already sprouted) for the cattle to eat.

Cutting of the bamboo takes place during the monsoon. Men have time to do it then and the bamboo is of better quality at this time, being softer and easier to mold. The new bamboo is used to

This eighteen-year-old Sherpa boy has carried so many heavy loads using the tump line that you can see the permanent indentation in his forehead. Porters are paid by the weight that they carry. Those who carry double loads (150 pounds) are paid double wages.

make trays and other useful objects, while last year's bamboo is cut for the shed roofs.

During the monsoon it can be raining on the mountain but not in the village, so no matter when the men go to cut the bamboo, it is probably raining. This makes life miserable. First of all, when the bamboo is cut, all the water on its leaves comes down and soaks the person cutting it. Then the leeches are out. They are everywhere and workers are constantly pulling leeches off of themselves. It is very uncomfortable to wear long pants for this job, so the workers' exposed legs and arms are wonderful targets. If a man is lucky enough to own socks and shoes, he becomes unlucky, because leeches crawl inside and bloat themselves. The men do not have to remove these leeches individually—as they pull off their socks the leeches fall away.

The mountain is very steep where the bamboo is cut for our village. It is impossible to carry the bamboo downhill, so the tops with leaves still intact are tied together and left to slide downhill. Of course, these bundles of about four hundred pieces of bamboo get caught up in everything. The men have to come along and untangle them—if they can—from trees and bushes. Sometimes trees must be cut down to free the bamboo. Other times the bamboo digs itself into the ground and must be dug out. When the bundle reaches an area that is not so steep, the leaves are cut off and the ends are trimmed. Then they are tied in two bundles of two hundred pieces each—the amount a man can then drag to the village, one bundle under each arm. The worker must also keep an eye to the weather. If it begins to rain heavily, he must be careful since he has to cross a small river to get home; if the waters rise, he will be trapped.

The forest also provides the raw material for making charcoal used by the blacksmiths. However, Sherpas are not blacksmiths. This is a job that is considered "untouchable." All blacksmiths are lowlanders. If you need something made or repaired, you wait until a traveling blacksmith comes to the village. Since the blacksmith will need charcoal, the villager makes it in anticipation of the blacksmith's coming. Blacksmiths are fed by the villagers, but they are never invited into Sherpa houses.

Our village does not get much food from the forest, although mushrooms are picked and some people pick the bamboo shoots to cook. Mama likes to cook nettles. Some of the plants of the forests are used as medicine. Everyone knows of the leaves that heal cuts (they are crushed and the juice is applied). There is a vine that when boiled and drunk helps to heal broken bones. There seems to be no herbal specialist in our village; most everyone knows the common cures. If someone gets seriously ill in the village, the village lama is first called in to say prayers. If the person does not get well, a *lhawa minung* (shaman) is consulted. If the person is still sick, then modern professional help is consulted. There is an aid post in the next village of Lukla, but the hospital with a real doctor is the whole way to Khunde, a distance of twenty miles. Going north, mostly uphill, the trek to the hospital is a three-day journey if the ill person is carried. Our own brother Mingma died in the village at the age of sixteen, because he was never taken to a hospital. Time just ran out. The lama and lhawa minung were consulted and then he died of white pustules in his mouth. Many of the deaths are this way. Even if the hospital were in the village, the families would still consult others and rely on forest medicines first.

If a person has an infected tooth, there is a woman in the village who is consulted. She will first heat a pencil-sized piece of metal until it is red hot. She then puts a piece of bamboo against the infected tooth and inserts the red-hot metal. This cures the infection. Infected eyes and ears are just left to run their natural course, and many people end up with loss of hearing and sight. My husband, when he was on trek, once had a spark from a fire go into his eye. It swelled and he could not see. The trekking company made him go to Kathmandu to the hospital where they covered his eye for three weeks; thankfully, he could see when the bandage was removed. He was lucky that he had no permanent damage.

Not all medicines, however, are Western or from the forest. When Phurba was very small, his grandfather's dog bit him on the arm. Mama squeezed her breast milk onto the wound to stop it from bleeding and to stop the swelling. It was then bandaged. It healed all right but left a nasty scar.

Ang Dawa, Phurba's next older brother, had his arm hurt from overwork. Mama took fat on her hand, held it above the fire until the fat turned warm and then rubbed Dawa's arm for over an hour with the fat.

Village life depends upon a sophisticated knowledge of climate, forest, and farming. People are secure in their houses, struggle with illness, and work hard on their land and tending their animals. Yet life in the village is certainly not easy. There are definitely harder ways to try to exist, but for someone from a Western country, it takes quite a bit of pace adjustment to be able to adapt to village life. In many ways it is a closer, easier relationship with family and others, and in many ways it is more difficult. There is no perfect place.

For me, a woman from Pennsylvania used to supermarkets, just the procurement of food was immensely complicated. And never had I dreamed about how life could flow around potatoes and their farming, the topic I next explore.

3

Pass the Shommar Sondu, Please

Sowing for a Harvest

The typical Sherpa farm is under ten acres. There is just not enough flat land available for one family to have more. Then there is the problem of labor. Since all the work is done by hand, a family can only do so much work.

The *riki* (potato), introduced in the nineteenth century, is the staple food. There are several types of potatoes planted. The *rikuma* (white potato) is very thin and long. The Sherpas also grow a yellow potato and red potato. In olden times they grew a black potato—it had very good taste but over the years it grew smaller and smaller until it was not worth planting. My husband's entire five-acre field is planted in potatoes. When they are harvested, they are laid out and the exterior allowed to dry, so that they will not rot. Then, with bamboo mats, four-foot-high walled circles are made in the storage part of the first floor of the house. Four or five of these will fit in the room. The circles are then filled with the potatoes. Once again this is to keep out moisture and prevent rotting. Like all farming, some years the crops are good and there are still potatoes left when the next year's crop is harvested; some years they run out months before the new crop.

The potatoes are planted at the end of February. In April, when the potatoes are about half grown, corn (introduced in the twentieth century) and beans are planted among them. After the potato is harvested in late June, buckwheat, wheat and barley are planted in its place. In a smaller garden the rest of the crops are grown: pumpkins, squash, carrots, plum tomatoes, cucumbers, cabbage, turnips, cauliflower, onions and garlic. These are the same crops that have been planted in the village for years and years. The villagers merely continue to plant the same thing. Each year seeds are taken from the ripe plants to start the planting the next year. Potatoes are saved and cut up, with an "eye" to each piece, to begin the new plants.

Millet is a crop that I often saw in other parts of Nepal; however, our village does not grow this plant. Phurba's mother tried to grow millet for several years, but it was too much trouble. It has to be sprouted in one location and then, during the monsoon, it must be transplanted into the larger field. When I visited other villages, I noticed entire fields of millet. The Sherpas make *tongba* (a mild alcoholic drink) from millet, but, of course, our village does not drink this because we do not grow its main ingredient.

The men's work is to plow the fields and make the necessary fences; the women then plant the crops and do all the weeding. While women tend and nurture the crops, men occupy themselves with the heavier work of wood collection, and so on.

There are two types of fertilizers that the village of Bhuwa/Shurkey uses. First is the bedding of dried leaves from the cattle. The Sherpas remove the leaves from a stable only when it is time to fertilize. They simply put down layer upon layer of foliage until spring and the time to fertilize arrives. This means that the leaves are sometimes three- or four-feet thick before they are removed. Then the leaves are dug up all at once. (Sometimes a Sherpa will place dried leaves directly on a field to achieve the same effect.) I was amazed that the stable did not smell as bad as those on typical American farms. It seems that the leaves soak up all the material and mask the smell.

The second type of fertilizer is obtained in the fall when lowlanders with sheep start making the rounds. The farmer puts up bamboo fences in a small area of his field which is now devoid of crops. The hundred or so sheep are herded into this small area and they eat all the weeds that have accumulated there while they fertilize the soil. Each day the farmer moves the fence and sheep until his entire farm has been covered.

The farmers have a system of *ngalok* (reciprocal work). When it comes time for harvesting and other heavy work, the villagers cooperate among themselves to complete the tasks. Whomever is having the work done that day provides food and drink for the workers. This system does not extend past our village. Though we have many relatives in the surrounding villages, we just do not have the time to help everyone.

In the summer, during the monsoon, if a man has all his other work done, he may work for the government widening trails, building bridges and participating in other such projects. Men are paid in wheat, oil, lentils, milk and other food stuffs. It is very hot, strenuous labor, but the Sherpas recognize the value it has for both the government and the people.

In a society that is so poor with so little surplus, servants are not expected, yet there is a means of providing extra labor in unusual circumstances. There is a twelve-year-old boy who lives and works with our friends, Pemba and Kami, at their trekking lodge. Pemba and Kami have three girls who are still too small to help with the chores. The boy is not a relative and Phurba is not sure where he came from, probably a poor family with too many children. Our other friends, Kanti and Pasang Rinzee, have Kanti's eighteen-year-old niece living with them. Her family lives a few days further south, and her father is a carpenter and lama who does not make enough to support his large family. Kanti takes care of four children—a son who attends school in Kathmandu, another son who is about twelve years old, a daughter of eight who is blind in one eye, and a toddler—and her husband's aged mother. Pasang Rinzee, was an alcoholic, and probably still is, though he is sick now, so Kanti could certainly use some extra hands to help.

Animal Ideas

Our village has cows and chickens. Goats, sheep and pigs are not good to have, as just a few of these animals eat everything in sight. If you want sheep, then you have just a hundred sheep and nothing else. Phurba once had one sheep. He played with it and it followed him no matter where he went in the village. Eventually it ate something poisonous and died. (Cows can eat poisonous plants and survive quite well, but sheep and goats die immediately.) Our village has no pastures for any animals, because all of the surrounding land is very steep. We are wedged between two very steep mountains with nowhere to go.

The Sherpas do not think of pigs as useful animals, as they provide no by-products. They eat dung and the people reason that this is not good for them. As in many societies long ago, pigs are not kept because they spoil so quickly after they are butchered. Trichinosis is carried by pigs, and though early people did not know this, they did learn that people died or got very sick from eating spoiled pork. I have seen black, hairy pigs in other parts of Nepal grubbing around in the sewer gutters of Pokhara and the garbage heaps of villages; it does not make me want to order *pork lo mein*.

Being Buddhists, the Sherpa do not kill any animals. Most animals are too important for their by-products to be killed. If an animal dies, the villagers will consume it unless it is obviously diseased. When a villager wants an animal butchered, he will wait for a non-Buddhist lowlander to come through the village. These lowlander men circulate through the area earning money as butchers. The Sherpa also obtain meat through lowland traders who walk the trails with their bamboo baskets full of butchered meat. If it is particularly hot weather, the Sherpas very carefully inspect the meat to make sure that it is not spoiled. Sometimes a lowlander will bring along a live sheep, goat or water buffalo and kill it when he finds sufficient villagers to warrant selling the whole animal. A little bit of meat goes a long way in the village—we purchased three buffalo ribs and fed the entire village of seventy adults with it!

Most villagers have chickens. They are easy to care for, multiply rapidly and supply eggs easily. Mama feeds the chickens with grain that has been used to make chang or *arak* (alcohol). When she clucks for the chickens, as farmers the world over know how to do, they come running from all corners of the farm. If you have a garden, it is wise to own chickens. They pick the bugs off the plants without damaging the tender leaves and stems. In a land of no pesticides, they keep the insects in check. Furthermore, chickens do not need special provisions, and they settle down in the stable at night with the cows.

The village has mostly black and white cows. Males are not desirable because they do not produce useful by-products. If one person in the village has a bull, then it services all the females. Sometimes someone comes through the village with a bull and rents him out. Female cows are also brought through the village for sale. A cow with a long tail is prized, and the Sherpa are sure to check the udder to make sure the cow looks healthy.

Cows spend the winter in the stable, but in the summer this is not very desirable. In the summer, when the crops are growing in the fields, the villagers erect a bamboo fence around the house to keep the cows away from the crops. In the fall, when everything has been harvested from the fields, the cows are staked out to eat the weeds and help fertilize.

Our village at 7,700 feet is not high enough to have yaks. However, some families of our village have occasionally owned yaks, letting them roam at higher altitudes. Yaks frequently pass through our village portering loads. Expeditions and trekking groups sometimes use yaks in the Khumbu instead of porters. The term *yak* is used by people of the West to refer to all of the many crossbreeds that exist. To the people of the Khumbu there are few true yaks, which refers only to the purebred male. The female is called a *knock*. They live at very high altitudes and like to stay above about 12,000 feet. If they are brought down too low for extended periods of time, they often die. They have thick coats of long shaggy hair that can be used to make blankets and sweaters. The Sherpas in the higher elevations have yaks, but their herds are not large because of the lack of fodder. In the summer the children take the yaks even higher to summer pastures, where there are small stone huts in which the children live. The children tend the yaks, carry dairy products back to their homes, make butter and cheese, and take care of their own daily needs. In the winter the yaks are kept in the villages but they must have abundant supplies of fodder.

The crossbreed *dzopkyo* is the product of a male yak and a cow. It is this animal that is most often seen in pictures. They do not have the thickness of hair or the extreme shagginess of the yak. The dzopkyo, weighing an average of 550 pounds, is the only animal that is used to haul loads. Most of the males have been castrated to make them more docile and easier to manage on trails and glaciers. Each animal can carry as much as 200 pounds. If a female is produced through the mating of a male yak and a cow, then it is called a *zum*. If they mate this zum with a regular bull (not a yak), then a *tole* (male) or *tolmu* (female) is produced. These are usually killed for meat immediately (but not by the Buddhist Sherpas, by a lowlander), as they are considered worthless and get very low prices if sold.

In our village no one knows how to make cheese. We are also located too far from a cheese factory to which we might take our milk. We use our milk to make *cheur* (yogurt) and *shoshem* (discussed on page 31).

Horses are thought to be an unnecessary luxury. There are none in Bhuwa/Shurkey and the only horse I remember seeing in the area belonged to the village headman for the area. I presume it was a status symbol. Horses are not kept because they do not produce useable by-products. Also, the people would never consider eating horse flesh, since they say they are like humans. When a horse dies, a lama must come and say the appropriate prayers and then the horse is thrown into the river. Plowing, often associated with horses, is done by the cows using a wooden plow tipped in metal. A fully metal plow would be too heavy for the cows to haul.

Our village also does not have water buffalo. It is too cold in the winter for them to survive. Besides, they eat too much, even though they do give more milk than a cow.

Dogs are an important part of every village. Our family has a *kez zongee* (best dog). Everyone from the surrounding villages wants one of our puppies. Our pair are very large black dogs with brown markings. They are not the true Himalayan mastiffs, but they are fierce and effectively fight bears. It is the job of the dogs to scare away all the various animals that come to raid the crops. The worst time is when the fields are ready for harvest. Then, to help the dogs, the children are sent to stay in *chya khang* (flimsy bamboo shelters) in the fields so that they can throw rocks at the various animals. If the winter is harsh, the wild animals may try to break into the food storage; dogs can prevent this. Of course, the farm animals are always preyed upon so fierce dogs are a desirable commodity.

One problem in the village is sleep. Everyone has dogs that bark all night long; light sleepers have a great deal of trouble. The dogs are worth the trouble, however, since they protect the commodities upon which the people depend.

Mice are as prevalent in the villages, as they are everywhere else. However, the Buddhist Sherpas do not set traps. To safeguard their grains they must make sure that they are sealed. Gaining plastic containers from the expeditions has helped this problem enormously. Still, in the small hours of the morning, while I lay awake in Mama's house, I could hear an occasional mouse scurrying among the roof beams. There are very few cats in the village. We have a cat, but it is not usually in the house.

Food from the Gods

Most Sherpas will take a little of the moisture from their food on their right ring finger and sprinkle it upward for the gods. This ritual is one of thanksgiving and is done with all liquid foods.

There are summer foods and winter foods. In summer, people eat what is ripening in the garden. Then they have well-balanced diets, full of good vegetables and fruits. In winter people must settle for what they can store. I found little evidence of preserving food. Some things, such as chilis, can be dried above the fire but the Sherpas have no salting or canning techniques. By the end of winter they are down to potatoes, flour and eggs. There are few fat Sherpas, except for my family. We are not rich but Mama is just naturally round and my sister-in-law has the fattest, roundest cheeks you have ever seen. As the boys grow up they are stockier than other Sherpas, but by no means fat.

Potatoes are the real staple of the diet. They are boiled with the skins on, then peeled and dipped in red-hot ground-up chilis for breakfast. It is a real eye opener. Potatoes are also fried, made into potato pancakes, and mashed with water and flour (*ril ducsan*).

Kami making ril ducsan (mashed potatoes). The boy working with him is not related but lives and works with Kami's family.

They like to eat this with a soup called *shommar sondu*. First they make *shommar* by taking sour milk and making it into butter. The leftover sour milk is then boiled until it clots. The clots are put in a bucket with some fresh milk and left for a couple of months to ferment. Then soup is made from the shommar using water, chilis and salt.

A similar food is shoshem, the scum from the inside of a milk bucket. This is mixed with chilis, water, and salt, fried in oil and put on the top of mashed potatoes. Phurba says this makes the potatoes taste very good. Without knowing it, I tried both these in the village but one small bite was enough for me. Maybe it is an acquired taste.

When the potatoes are harvested, they are in a variety of sizes. The tiny ones, about the size of a thumb nail, are taken to the river and washed very well. Then they are put on a flat rock and crushed with a wooden mallet. The crushed potatoes are left there to dry. If the sun is very bright, it will probably take from two to three weeks for them to dry. Because of the animals and birds, someone must sit and watch the potatoes during the day, and they must be gathered each night and taken to the house. This is a job left to the very young or the very old. When the potatoes are dry, they are ground at the mill into flour. This potato flour is then mixed with buckwheat flour and added to boiling water until a gooey mass is made. This is then eaten with soup.

Tsampa (a dough made from roasted barley flour) is eaten with soup. Mama roasts the barley and then takes it down to the stream to be ground by a small set of stones. Our stream, the Shurkey Khola, branches into the river Dudh Kosi (these are Nepalese words not Sherpa ones). The Shurkey Khola is not very wide, though during the monsoon it swells greatly. A small side stream has been routed to the grist mill; the small shed houses two rocks. The water turns one rock against the fixed other rock. Mama drops the grain in a hole in the top rock and the flour comes out the sides. She mixes the barley flour with a little water until it has the consistency of dough. This is then placed on a plate and the people scoop up little amounts with their fingers. Few people use cutlery in the village. They have it, and I was always given a knife, fork and spoon, but most people use their fingers. Soup is drunk out of the bowls. With their right hand (no lefts, please; they are unclean), they roll the tsampa into a ball and press their thumb into the dough making a small hollow. This they then use to scoop up soup, usually water, chilis and salt. One day when my stomach was not feeling well Mama hand fed me tsampa. It has a slightly nutty flavor and did seem to settle my stomach.

Flour is made into *chappatis* (flat unleavened bread), toasted on stones by the fire and eaten in a variety of ways. My husband's favorite way to prepare chappatis is to fry potatoes, chilis and a leafy green vegetable, similar to spinach, and then, roll this into the chappati. Tibetan bread is also eaten; it consists of a braided dough, made from wheat flour, which is then fried in oil.

Wandering merchants sell water buffalo meat which can be made into *moomoos*, small dumplings with spices inside a dough ball. These are dipped in more spices before being eaten.

Cque is made by boiling flour and salt together. It is drunk like soup. Millet flour cque fills you up but corn flour cque does not.

Thukpa is a noodle-based stew. *Tho* is a tuber which grows wild. It is gathered, boiled, ground up (as when making mashed potatoes), and then buckwheat flour is added to it. The cook then rivels it, or twirls the dough between the palms of the hands until small strings emerge. These are dropped into boiling water. Phurba tells me that one should swallow the rivels whole because if they are chewed they will make the throat burn.

A variety of other foods is available. Eggs are preferred raw, or mixed raw with cooked potatoes. Eggs are also made into omelets. Sherpa stew is a variety of vegetables with potatoes and meat, if meat is available. Many meals are vegetarian, since it is expensive to buy meat. Noodles are both bought and made. *Daal bhaat* (lentils and rice) is a favorite. In our village the rice must be bought from the lowlanders. The lentils are stewed until they have cooked down the water to a gooey paste. This is cooked with a great deal of chilis. The *daal* (lentils) is then poured over the *bhaat* (rice). These are Nepalese words the Sherpas have borrowed. The Nepalese have various names to describe rice in all its forms: rice in the field, seed rice, rice in the store, uncooked rice, cooked rice, and so on. I have not found daal bhaat to my liking. To me it is just a very sticky mass that is so highly spiced that it burns my mouth for hours afterward.

Garlic is a seasoning that is much desired in the village. The people think it makes foods taste very good; therefore, much garlic is added. They also believe that the higher one goes in altitude, the more garlic the person should eat. It supposedly helps to guard against altitude sickness; hence, garlic is used a great deal on trekking and expeditions to safeguard the foreigners.

The Sherpas do not have a great deal of flavorings; garlic, chilis, butter and salt make up the majority of what they use. The butter they churn themselves; they do not add salt as we do. Salt is gained in trade. It used to come from Tibet. Today a housewife buys a lump of salt from a traveling merchant. She breaks it off and crushes it in her mortal and pestle. This produces various-sized crystals of salt. Some are very large and rather detract from the flavor of the food (and make for much crunching).

Fruits that can be found in the village are apples, peaches and strawberries. The strawberries grow wild and are considerably smaller than commercially produced berries. Other fruits, such as limes, lemons, mangoes, bananas, tangerines, and so on, are sometimes brought up the trails for sale.

There are two ways that outside goods come into the village. Lone traders wander from village to village until they have sold everything, at which time they return home. Almost everything they carry is food. Traders do not usually take lodgings; they sleep outside or on someone's porch, which costs about one rupee. The second way goods arrive is on market day. A group of traders travel together in a set pattern. Thursday is market day in Bhuwa/Shurkey. The traders either stay overnight close to the village or in the village, as the market is at first light. Then the traders continue up the trail to Lukla for market day, which is on Thursday also. The next day is a travel day for them, and market day in Nauche/Namche Bazaar is on Saturday.

The most famous drink of the area is Tibetan tea. The people drink a good deal of regular tea in the mornings. Most mornings I had three cups at least. We drank tea, did chores, washed up, and then ate breakfast (potatoes) about two to three hours after rising. The tea is always served with lots of milk and sugar. They like it steaming hot and keep it in a Thermos bottle—the old type with the cork. Tibetan tea has butter and salt added. The tea, milk, butter and salt (no sugar) is churned in a butter churn and then put back on the fire to boil again. It is a drink that I could tolerate if I thought of it as soup, but one cup was enough, as it is very fatty and oily.

The main alcoholic drink of the Sherpas is chang, or beer. It can be made from any grain or potatoes. The grain is boiled—the people prefer that only the family is present, since others may cast an evil eye on the brew—and then spread out on mats to dry. Yeast and a small piece of charcoal are mixed in a bucket with the grain (the charcoal is also for the evil eye). In three to four days it begins to smell. Then it is put into a barrel—wooden in the old days, but today the people use the plastic clothes barrels they have gotten from the expeditions. (The plastic is slightly dangerous since it can explode during the fermenting process.) The top is sealed very tightly and it can be kept six to seven months. Usually the mixture is kept sealed for two to three weeks. Chang that has been aged four to five weeks is very strong. After six to seven months it must be able to blow your socks off! After it has fermented, the grain is mixed with boiled water in a bamboo sieve, and the solids are funneled out. The women squeeze the grain to remove the excess water and add boiled water two to three times. After the process has been completed, the grain is fed to the dogs or chickens (nothing is wasted in Sherpa society). If the fermented grain should happen to spoil, it can be turned into *arak* (grain alcohol, rakshi in Nepalese). Chang can be thick or thin depending on the amount of water added, and it is white in color.

Chang drinking has become part of the Sherpa religion. At every event that the village lama oversees, chang must be drunk. Any building project must have chang, as must the erection of prayer flags, or the hiring of workmen. It is customary to offer chang to a guest. If a family does not do so, it is an unconscionable breach of etiquette. The guest is pressed to drink with the words "*Shay, shay,*" (drink, drink), said three times. Each time the guest drinks, the cup or glass is refilled. In our village chang is served in china teacups on special occasions; on normal occasions it is served in glasses. I was almost always given a teacup. Many Sherpas worry about being given poison in the chang. Phurba's great-grandfather was poisoned with chang by relatives. It was too long ago for Phurba to remember why.

Fighting often occurs when the people drink too much. There are certain times of the year when there is very little to do in the village: December, January, February and August. Then the chang drinking is at its worst. The people have little to entertain them, so they wander from house to house drinking chang. They claim it also keeps them warm, though science says that alcohol takes blood away from the skin surface and therefore should make them colder.

At times, it can be said that the Sherpa also drink too much arak, the grain alcohol of the mountains. Arak in our village seemed to be drunk a little less than chang. One February, in preparation for Losar, the Sherpa New Year, my brothers-in-law made arak. They put a large earthen pot on the fire and filled it with mash. The mash may be made of corn, millet, rice, potatoes or the sour chang mixture. A second earthen pot was placed on top of the first one. It had holes in the bottom. The crack between the two pots was plastered shut with cow dung. A small earthen pot to catch the drippings was set inside this second pot. A brass pot filled with cold water was then placed on top of the second pot. The seal between the earthen pot and the brass pot was made with a strip of cloth. As the mash boiled and evaporated, it condensed on the brass pot and dripped into the small earthen pot.

Every time the water got hot, it was replaced with cold water. That meant that we had an abundance of hot water. The boys all took baths, the family washed clothes, and Mama washed pots and pans that had only seen a cold-water wash for weeks before. Brother Mingma scoured the outside of the blackened pots with corn shocks until they became shiny clean.

Sanchung is another type of beer that is made. Corn or millet flour is added to boiling water and mixed. It is cooled for one hour and then spread on plastic until it is just warm. Yeast is added and the mixture is put in a pot with a cloth around it and the top sealed. This is left for three or four days and then put into a barrel for two more days. Water is added and three days later it is ready to serve, at which time more water is added and the drink is mixed with a whisk common in the village (a piece of bamboo with another piece attached at the bottom to make a T). The whisk is held between the palms and is rubbed back and forth to twirl the stick. Then the sanchung is ready to drink.

The work of preparing food and drink can be an enormous task. Consider a day I spent with Pemba. Pemba and Kami own the most prosperous trekking lodge in the village (there are three altogether). In the great earthquake several years ago their house and lodge had slid down the hill and they had to have another one erected. After several years of saving money, they were ready to make the dormitory room on the second floor into individual rooms. Kami went to his forestland and cut trees for the boards. He hired Sherpa carpenters to saw the logs into boards, plane them down and erect the walls. My sister-in-law, Pasang Phuti, married one of these carpenters.

The men of the village returning with wood for Pemba and Kami's lodge. Kami has cut the wood and left it to dry; the men then perform reciprocal work (ngalok) by hauling the wood to the village. Kami will, in turn, help each man carry his wood. The men hauled four loads that day and received all their meals at the lodge. Leaves are stored in the shed along the trail, to be fed to the cows when fodder runs out.

It was Pemba and Kami's responsibility to feed these men for the weeks that it took them to do the work. Pemba had quite a time of it. One evening seven New Zealanders had stopped at the lodge and had eaten supper there. The next morning Pemba first fed her family and the carpenters. Then the New Zealanders ate breakfast and left. At about eight in the morning the ten village men who were to haul firewood for the lodge arrived for breakfast. Pemba served them boiled potatoes. Each man carried four loads of wood that day in the bamboo baskets held by tump lines. Each time they returned they had chang to drink. Pemba fed the carpenters, the wood carriers and her family lunch, including chang, which had to be made. Then they all ate supper.

We were there for lunch and supper, as Phurba was helping Kami work that day. Pemba had an incredible amount of work to do, just with the cooking. She managed it all with a huge smile and

Phurba in Pemba's kitchen showing her shelves containing dishes and foodstuffs. Sunglasses are the ultimate status symbol.

much talking and teasing. While she prepared the meals, she took care of her children, tended to the house, and entertained other visitors. I wished I could have helped her more than I did, but I had no idea then how to do the simplest tasks and showing me would have taken longer than doing the task herself. I helped by occupying the tiny children.

Days of the People

The Sherpas do not have a calendar like in Western societies. Losar (New Year) occurs in our month of February. Their months are determined according to the lunar cycle, beginning approximately on our twelfth of each month. It is the village lama who possesses the *Dhadur* (Tibetan book of dates). This book shows when each month begins according to the first day of the full moon. The lama then counts thirty days until the next month begins. However, if the first day of the full moon cycle does not occur on that day, then a double day must be counted. If the full moon occurs before the full thirty-day count, then the lama skips from day number six to day number eight. The *Dhadur* has the day's horoscope listed after each day. The villagers consult the lama for the right days to begin house building, marriage and so on. Most villagers rely on the lama to inform them of exactly what day it is, since they do not have calendars.

The names of the months are as follows:

Dawa Thangpo	February/March	potato planting
Dawa Ngiwa	March/April	corn planting, wood cutting
Dawa Sumbu	April/May	carrying firewood, hoeing
Dawa Siwa	May/June	field tending
Dawa Ngawa	June/July	potato digging, planting
Dawa Thukpa	July/August	field tending
Dawa Dyunwa	August/September	corn picking
Dawa Gyepa	September/October	trekking
Dawa Chiwa	October/November	trekking, wood cutting
Dawa Chyuchikpa	November/December	work in house
Dawa Chungiwa	December/January	work in house
Dawa Chuchikpa	January/February	carrying manure, plowing

Dawa, literally means "moon," but in this context it is also taken for month. The words following *Dawa* mean first, second, third and so on. Therefore, *Dawa Thangpo* is first month, *Dawa Ngiwa* is second month, and on to twelfth month.

Despite the month, there is seasonal work allowing life to continue as it always has. Whether a person is farming, exploiting the forest, tending animals, preparing food, or doing any of the myriad other tasks, all is done in the family for the family.

4

Of Animals,
Seen and Unseen

I sat completely still, breathing shallowly as my father had taught me while watching turkeys in the Pennsylvania woods. A tiny pika crept out of a small crack in a huge mound of rocks. It paused, like it was cast in iron. For five minutes it stayed immobile. Then it quickly raced across a piece of rock ledge. Suddenly a shadow passed over the ledge. The pika froze again. High above circled a hawk. The pika (and I) sat for fifteen minutes without moving—a more remarkable feat for me than for the pika. When the tiny creature was finally assured that the shadow had gone away, it quickly disappeared back into the crack in the rocks. What a delightful twenty minutes for me. The trails of Nepal are highways, and with constant traffic the wild animals learn to stay away from them. I had ambled up a little-used side trail at the end of a hard day and sat down for some solitude. The reward I had received was unexpected and heartwarming. I had wanted to take the furry little creature home with me. Unfortunately, not all of the creatures of the mountains are quite as nice.

Like all country areas the Khumbu has a variety of wild animals. The villagers are most concerned with the ones that intrude into their lives and income. Bears—black bears—are probably the worst. They can destroy an entire farm in one evening. They eat everything in sight and tear up what they do not eat. That is why the villagers all have ferocious dogs.

There used to be a man in the village who was 104 years old—and who had a flintlock rifle probably as old as he. This man was surprised one day by a bear and ironically dropped his gun. The bear, being quite as surprised as the old man, tumbled down a hill.

39

The old man went after the bear and gave him a good kick. I cannot help but admire the grit of the fellow, though I question his wisdom, as the bear turned around and killed him.

The Khumbu is home to a number of less-threatening animals, but which, nonetheless, cause problems for the Sherpa. *Remmun* (weasels) kill chickens and suck out their blood and the *gyipchung* (fox) will kill chickens, goats and eat corn. There are also wolves or jackals (also called gyipchung), and because they are larger they are able to kill the cattle. The *rongpishur* (porcupine) will eat corn. Since they are impossible to attack physically (because of their quills), the boys throw pumpkins or squash at any intruder until its quills are embedded in the food. This then immobilizes the animal so that the boys can throw rocks at it to kill it. I thought such animal killing conflicted with their Buddhist beliefs; but if it is go hungry or kill, they will kill.

When Phurba was thirteen or fourteen years old his family had many goats. One night one was killed and, when Phurba went looking for it, he found a trail of blood and a *zik* (snow leopard) dragging the goat away. I brought out the *National Geographic* with the story about the snow leopards of western Nepal and showed Phurba the pictures. Yes, he said that was the creature that he saw. I did not know there were snow leopards in the Khumbu; evidentally there were in 1978.

Rkik (red monkeys) and *hraka* (monkeys with white heads and tails), both in the langur family, roam up and down the mountains. They will attack a farm in troops and eat the wheat. Red squirrels will open every ear of corn and only eat one or two kernels. The crop is then destroyed if moisture enters the open ears. Phurba, as a child, had killed squirrels with a slingshot, but the family would not eat them. Crows will pick all the new corn plants out of the ground, but they do not eat anything.

There are a variety of other animals in the surrounding forests, which do not seem to harm the farms: barking deer, spotted deer, *goral* (the Nepalese word for a small wild goat), wild boar, civet cats and red pandas, among others. The *nigalya ponya* (red panda) is a bamboo eater like its larger cousin. It is a small animal but has the gait of a bear. I was greatly impressed when Phurba said that he had seen red pandas, but rather disturbed to find that he did not think anything of them being so rare. To the people it does not matter how rare an animal is; what matters is whether or not it harms crops.

In the higher elevations, up toward Nauche/Namche Bazaar, there are *tahr* (great brown mountain goats). I have seen musk deer tracks right outside of Phortse. Phurba tells me of an animal he calls *lha* which hops. He calls it a kangaroo in English. Despite my research, I can find no evidence of kangaroos in Nepal or of what this animal might be. However, the government of Nepal has restricted the killing of this animal.

Almost everyone thinks of Yeti when the Himalayas or the Sherpas are mentioned. Phurba says that none have ever been as low as his village. He does not see any reason to believe or disbelieve that the Yeti exist. He has never seen one, though he has seen the purported skull of one in the Khumjung *gonda* (monastery, *gompa* in Nepalese) and the scalp and hand in the Pangboche *gonda*.

The word *Yeti* comes from *ye* (rock) and *te* (animal). I spent a fascinating morning's tea in the village of Khumjung with Khonjung Chungbe, one of the most famous men of the area. This marvelous elderly gentleman toured the world in the early 1960s with Sir Edmund Hillary trying to prove the existence of the Yeti. He has a wonderful photo album of pictures showing him with famous people such as John F. Kennedy and Queen Elizabeth II. His stories are intriguing. According to this experienced sojourner, the Yeti has red hair so many people mistake it for a Buddhist nun, and there are several varieties, one larger than the other. Khonjung Chungbe believes that it carries off children, sometimes to eat them, and one had supposedly been sighted right outside Khumjung just days before I was there. He made the stories seem so real as he crouched over, hands hanging loose, and told his tale. Years later Phurba, upon seeing an orangutan in the Philadelphia Zoo, immediately said, "Yeti."

Other sources say that there are three different types of Yeti. The first—*chhuti*—are not harmful to humans but will carry off cattle and pet animals. The second—*miti*—are very harmful to humans. The third—*chhelma*—are thought of as forest shamans (Kunwar 1989). There are stories of Yeti carrying people away and returning them. They are usually females and are not killed. These women supposedly live in the caves with the Yetis and are then returned to the exact spot from which they were abducted one year later.

Almost as many stories are told of tigers, an intrinsic part of the India subcontinent. They are not seen in the Khumbu, though they might have been there since parents still frighten their children by saying that the tiger will carry them away if they are bad. Dreaming of a tiger means that God is not pleased with you. A woman born in the year of the tiger will not find a husband easily, since it is believed that her husband would soon die. However, a man born in the year of the tiger is thought to be bold, strong and powerful.

Although I am not much of a bird fancier, there is one unusual bird of the Himalayas that intrigues me—the *lammergeyer*

Khonjung Chungbe, who in the early 1960s travelled the world with Hillary trying to prove the existence of the Yeti. I had morning tea with Khonjung Chungbe and his family in Khumjung and listened to his fascinating stories. (It seems that only the older men wear these traditional garments.)

(*Gypaetus barbatus*). It is a huge, golden vulture with a wingspan of up to nine feet. It has tassels of spiny black feathers hanging from its nostrils and a black mask across its eyes. It is wonderful to watch them float on the air currents around the mountains. It is especially fascinating when they are actually circling beneath where you are standing on the trail. Lammergeyers are distinctive because they have learned to take bones up in the air and drop them on rocks to crack them so that they can get at the marrow. I have recently heard reports from trekkers in the Annapurna region that the lammergeyers have taken to swooping down on tents and tearing them open in hopes of finding food. The story did come out of the region during a particularly bad stretch of winter weather, perhaps explaining the behavior.

For a Westerner it would be a dream come true to study some of these exotic animals, but, to the natives of the area, most of them are just nuisances. To preserve a rare species often means sacrifices for the locals that they just do not understand. When people live intimately with the forest—its bounties and its threats—there is an attitude toward flora and fauna that insulated Westerners cannot easily understand.

5

Living

Present and Past

As expeditions and trekkers gave away clothing, Sherpa men adopted the cast-offs. As a result, native dress was gradually abandoned. The women have not made this change. Sherpa women still wear the *angi* (long gown). These are usually made of wool, though today they tend to be a wool and polyester blend. The preferred colors are dark blues, browns and blacks with a white pin stripe. Under these, the women wear a variety of blouses. The *syamjar* (traditional blouse) flaps over in the front but does not button. These are still worn on special occasions, though in everyday life you can see everything from T-shirts to western blouses. The gown also overlaps and is held in place by a *matril* (apron). These are always decorated with multi-colored stripes reflecting Tibetan origins. The Tibetan women refugees who have entered Nepal in the last thirty years all wear the same apron. If the family can afford it, a belt with a gigantic *kyetee* (silver buckle) is cinched around the waist. If the dress is too long, the woman doubles it up at the waist before tying on the apron.

One time Phurba and I were extremely extravagant and brought Mama not only a wool angi but also one made of jade green brocade with a magenta blouse. She was so pleased. It was Losar when new clothing is typically worn and really made her feel special, as indeed she is to us. Phurba tried the dresses on in the tiny shop at Bodnath, a Tibetan settlement outside Kathmandu. I

Pemba in the doorway to her shop at the Thamserku Lodge with her three daughters. You can see some of the items for sale on the shelves in the background. Notice Pemba's silver buckle (kyetee) and multi-colored apron (matril). She is wearing the watch I gave to her. The children's Western clothes were brought back from Kathmandu by their father, Kami, when he was shopping after an expedition.

had to stifle giggles. He did not seem to think it was odd at all for a man to measure up his mother's dress.

Small children run naked most of the summer. They swim in the river but must be careful because of the currents. The river can swell from a small, lazy flowing stream in the winter to a crashing, dangerous river in the monsoon.

Most Sherpas have few changes of clothing. Clothing is worn until it literally falls apart. It is passed down from older to younger siblings. Since farm work is so dirty, the people constantly appear filthy. Washing clothing in the cold rivers is not an easy task and beating clothing on a rock wears it out all the quicker. Clothing is difficult to dry in the monsoon. In the winter clothes can be hung in the house, but they take so long to dry that they would be as dirty from the dust and smoke as before they were washed. Sherpas do wash clothes, but they are not clean fanatics.

Some Sherpas never bathe. This is true of primarily the older people (those over fifty). Oftentimes, especially in winter, people say bathing could cause colds and pneumonia. The attitude and beliefs remind me of colonial times when the spring and fall baths were the only ones people took. Today, with the influence of outsiders, the younger generation is much more regular in their bathing habits. In the villages the Sherpa usually do not go to the extreme of carrying water from the river, heating it and then bathing. They bathe in a river that flows with glacial water and is frigidly cold. Women strip down to a sort of slip that they wear; men go into the cold, running water in their underwear or naked. They try to find secluded areas for, if someone spots them, they will be laughed at, and knowing Sherpas, probably soon everyone else in the village will hear of their embarrassment.

Sherpa men have very little facial hair. Some never need to shave, others shave very infrequently. My father-in-law used to pull out the few hairs he had. Phurba always had himself shaved when he was in Kathmandu; it cost about ten cents. It was quite a letdown for Phurba when I had to teach him to shave himself after we moved to the United States.

Women can be seen sitting in the sun picking the lice out of each other's hair. Afterward they apply a new coating of oil to the hair and rebraid it without washing it. If it is a special occasion, they braid in a piece of red yarn with a tassel on the end. Inside the house women's heads are usually bare, but, when they go outside, they like to wear something—an old towel that is gathered in the back and tucked in is standard in our village.

Fleas are a problem in the village. Cleanliness is not so much the problem as the fact that there are so many animals. The dogs are infested with fleas. Even though they are never allowed inside

the houses the fleas still make it in. The winter frees the people of
the torment of fleas, since the inside of a house is usually as cold
as outside. Phurba tells me of having fleas as a child, they hide in
the doubled up areas of clothing and where the body is warmest.
Additionally, the fleas get into the thick cotton blankets and wreak
havoc with sleep. Cleanliness of body and clothing can usually keep
them off people.

Shoes are a somewhat rare commodity. Many people have flip-
flops. Some of the women wear high top basketball sneakers, when
they can get them.

The Sherpas live in a strange combination of past and present
times. The boy next door is playing a tape of Michael Jackson, but
in contrast, feminine hygiene products are not obtainable in
Kathmandu, much less in the villages. Sherpa women do what
women have done down through history until the twentieth
century; they use rags. These are then washed out to be used again
next month. So if the basics are not available, one can guess that
the Sherpas have never even heard of all the other products that
we have here in the West for feminine hygiene. I wonder how I
would go about describing some of these products. I can imagine
the reaction I would get; the ladies would cover their mouths with
their hands and laugh hysterically. Phurba was completely
mystified when I tried to explain tampons.

I have often seen women, especially, covering their mouths
when they laugh. In the United States people used to do the same
thing because they had bad teeth, but the Sherpa's teeth are
beautiful. My husband has pearly white, incredibly hard teeth. He
can chew the unpopped kernels of popcorn like they were nothing.
The biggest problem with teeth is plaque. Though many people
brush their teeth, no one ever gets teeth cleaned. So beautiful,
perfect teeth can fall out of diseased gums.

Marriage and Family

In the old days all Sherpa marriages were arranged by the
families. Today this practice can still be found in some of the far-
flung villages. Mostly men who have been on trek—that is, who have
gone to Kathmandu and been influenced by Western ideas—no
longer let their families choose for them. However, the old ideas still
hang over their heads when they go looking for a bride. Who is this
woman? Who is her family? Do they own anything worthwhile?

When the choice is made, the boy's relatives go to the girl's
parents to ask consent. They bring chang with them. If the girl's
father drinks the chang, he accepts the boy. After awhile grain is

sent to the bride's house. Then the groom's relatives go to the bride's house to fix a date for the wedding. The bride's maternal uncle should be present. They bring arak, rice pudding, fried potatoes, meat, eggs and bread. The bride's family offers them chang in return.

The village lama can perform the *gengu* (marriage ceremony). The proper prayers are said and butter is smeared on the foreheads of the bride and groom. They then bow to their opposite kinship groups. The wedding is followed by a big party with lots of chang, singing and dancing. No gifts are given to the couple; however, the day after the wedding the bride gives all her husband's relatives chang and they put money in her dress. The bride then goes to live with her husband. In the old days, when children of ten and eleven were often married, the bride would stay at her home until she matured.

Each Sherpa belongs to a patrilineal clan with a common remembered ancestor. They practice clan exogamous marriage. My husband's clan is called Salika and they cannot marry anyone else in that clan, nor can they marry anyone in their mother's clan.

In some parts of the world people practice the levirate or the sororate (a man marrying his brother's widow or a widower marrying his unmarried sister-in-law). This is common where land or other economic resources are scarce; the reason given for these practices is so that there will not be many children among whom to split up the limited resources (most likely land). This is not necessary in the Khumbu, since most families have multiple fields that are distributed to the sons. Some sons are now moving to Kathmandu and not taking farms in the villages.

It seems that some polyandry and polygyny existed in the old days. In polyandry, two brothers shared one wife. Reasons for this ranged from a lack of women in the area to a lack of money in the family. Polygyny is outlawed in Nepal, though it still exists in the mountains. I stayed in a house in Phortse where a man had two wives. Today, the usual reason for such plural marriages is that the first wife cannot produce children. Since children are so vital, a man either has to divorce her, and then no one else would want to marry her, or take another wife. Sometimes the second wife is a sister to the first (sororal polygyny). That is believed to make life a little easier, since sisters already presumably can get along with each other. My mother-in-law's sister's husband has also married a Swiss woman. He lives in Switzerland, returns very infrequently to Nepal, leaves his Swiss wife in Kathmandu, and then goes to the village and gives his first wife money.

I also know of a Tamang man who has a Tamang wife in his village and a Sherpa wife who lives in Kathmandu. I find it significant that the Sherpa wife does not live in his village, where she probably would not be accepted by the Tamangs, nor does she live in her own village, where she would probably no longer be accepted by her family. She is a beautiful, pleasant woman who makes money by supplying Sherpas with food and lodging. Often the men from the villages come to Kathmandu to get trekking jobs. They search out places such as this woman's where they can be fed Sherpa food cheaply and sleep on her floor. We often visited her when we were in town. Her two young children kept me entertained for hours. She had a tiny kitchen and a long, narrow eating, living, and sleeping room. In trekking season there would usually be so many men there that it would be hard to find a place on the floor to sleep.

Husbands and wives are considered equal in Sherpa society. Sherpa women express their ideas often and vocally. One old woman in the village, upon finding her husband drunk at two o'clock in the afternoon, proceeded to scold him forcefully in front of everyone and then dragged him bodily from the house as he fought along the way. The rest of the people in the room laughed uproariously.

Women sit on the floor in the houses while the men sit on the *nyuthi* (benches). Men and women do not mingle socially; women and children gather together and the men gather somewhere else. Men and women do not hold hands or ever kiss in public either; they share their lives at home but outside they are apart. I found this especially true in my case. Phurba's friends were shy around me, because I was a woman and a foreigner. His best friend, Kami, would not even look at me. I thought that he did not like me for the longest time until Phurba assured me he was merely shy.

Ultimogeniture is the rule in Sherpa society. This is where the youngest son inherits the farmhouse and half of the main fields, and he must then take care of his aged parents. The older sons bring their wives home until the youngest is old enough to be married; then they move out on their own to other fields the family owns. If there are a number of sons, then one of the middle sons can be sent to a monastery.

The old are not worthless. There are still many tasks that they can do, when they are unable to work in the fields. Baby-sitting is an important job, freeing the younger women to work. Household work, repairs and religious duties can take up their time. If they live along a well-traveled trail, the older people often sell jewelry and other items or take care of a very small store. The Sherpa have no special term of respect for older people, but they are treated well. One woman in our village was 105 years old. On trek Phurba was once given a pair of lady's pull-on sneakers. Of course, they did not fit and he did not want them. He could have given them to his mother or sister, but the elderly lady had no shoes and so he gave them to her. This is an appropriate act of respect toward the aged.

Children are the lifeblood of any community. Sherpa children usually are named after the day of the week on which they were born. Each day has its own symbol attached to it, an important consideration for other life events.

Day	Sherpa Name	Symbol	Additional Symbols
Sunday	Nima	Fire	Sun
Monday	Dawa	Water	Moon
Tuesday	Mingma	Fire	
Wednesday	Lhakpa	Water	
Thursday	Phurba	Wind	
Friday	Pasang	Earth	
Saturday	Pemba	Earth	

These names and symbols are also taken into consideration when marriage is about to take place, though not as much today as in the recent past. There are certain combinations that are good, such as our own: Phurba's Thursday wind is known to go quite nicely with my Tuesday fire.

Other Sherpa names vary. Since there are so many Phurba's around, people tend to call everyone by the first and middle names. However, since there are also some Phurba Gelzen's around, sometimes the name has to be qualified by saying from Bhuwa/Shurkey. Sherpas do not use Sherpa as their last name. When my husband went for his passport he had to have a last name, so the government official wrote down Sherpa. Sherpa women are called Sherpani. When I tried to explain to him that married people in the United States both have the same last name with *Mr.* and *Mrs.* in front, he was completely mystified. It took him quite sometime to accept that this was the way that it was done here. Sherpa names can also be altered. Pemba can be Temba, Pertemba or Penoorie, Dawa can go to Dali, and Annumay can be generated from Nima.

Phurba has four brothers: Ang Dawa, Mingma Norbu (deceased), Lhakpa Gelu and Nha Temba. Nha means fifth (boy) child. Phurba also has two sisters: Pasang Phuti and Nang Lamu (deceased). I have read other sources that maintain that most Sherpa brothers do not get along because of much rivalry. This does not seem to be the case in Bhuwa/Shurkey or the surrounding villages. All our brothers seem to get along beautifully with much

Phurba and his brothers (left to right): Phurba Gelzen, Ang Dawa, Nha Temba, Lhakpa Gelu. All are wearing new clothes from the U.S.

love. There is an occasional village family that fights, but that can be found anywhere.

A naming ceremony takes place one week after a child's birth. An eight- or nine-year-old boy goes early in the morning and cuts a pine tree. He cuts the bottom branches off, and, in the middle of the tree, he puts a white cloth holding rice, corn and wheat. If the baby is a boy, the tree is put outside the house on the right side of the door; if the baby is a girl, it is placed on the left side. The village lama comes and says prayers and everyone gets chang.

Sherpas have the same symbols for years as the Chinese. A person's symbol is determined by the year of his or her birth. The symbols are in a circle cycle as follows:

    1990—Horse
    1991—Sheep
    1992—Monkey
    1993—Rooster

1994—Dog
1995—Hog
1996—Rat
1997—Ox
1998—Tiger
1999—Rabbit
2000—Dragon
2001—Snake
2002—Horse
2003— Sheep
2004—Monkey
Etc.

Certain combinations are better than others. For example, it is good for a man to be a snake or dragon. Phurba is a snake and I am a hog.

Birthing and Childhood

There are no midwives in our village and women rarely go to the hospital for a birth. Women who have been through childbirth know what to do and help each other through labor. Once Mama had to wash her arm very thoroughly and turn a baby around inside the mother; she was successful. No young children are allowed in the room when a birth is taking place, as they could get sick from observing it. No visitors are allowed in, as they could give the mother the evil eye. The husband is usually not present; he is probably drinking chang with the boys. After the birth, the mother drinks chang and two to three pounds of melted butter to give her back her strength. Sherpa women drink as much chang during pregnancy as they do at any other time. It may be one of the reasons babies are often born with low birth weights. Poor diet, strenuous labor, poor sanitation and smoke in the houses are obviously some of the other reasons. The women do not make any connection between any of these and their unborn child.

If a married woman does not get pregnant, the village lama may be called to pray or a shaman may be consulted. Some people go to Dharmasol—a large temple in the Solu, which is a six-day walk to the south of Bhuwa/Shurkey—and pray for children. No one in our village does this, however, since the temple is so far away. My husband has no faith in it either, which may indicate another reason why the people in our village do not espouse this practice. Furthermore, the people do not consult doctors for such things as fertility drugs, and other advanced methods are not available. The Sherpas look at multiple births as being unnatural. Twins are sometimes born but more than that is extremely rare—virtually unheard of. They believe that animals have litters, not humans. If a mother were to have three or four children at once, they probably would all be so small that they would die. Even with twins, the weaker one often dies. Nepal has a mortality rate of 106 out of 1,000 live births (World Almanac 1992); I suspect the figures are even higher for the mountains.

In Sherpa society children are greatly loved. Boys are thought to be no better than girls; but families want boys for their labor. Older children are not treated better or worse than the younger. Perhaps this is because of the high mortality rate. Sherpa children seem to be well disciplined. If they do something wrong, they are punished, usually a pat on the rear. They are obviously loved, as they climb from one adult lap to another and are talked to and treated kindly by everyone. They are taught from the first that they are not to make loud noises in the houses and not to interrupt adults. Therefore, sitting around someone's kitchen with children all about is delightful. When outside the children do not seem to be very noisy either.

I found only one exception to this. One young fellow in our village was throwing fits, screaming and yelling every time I ran across him. I do not think it was my influence, however; he appeared to be developmentally disabled. This happens everywhere, of course. We have one middle-aged man in the village who is deaf, dumb and developmentally impaired; he is unmarried.

In former times many cretins were born in Sherpa society because of the great lack of iodine in the Sherpa diet, as evidenced by many goiters. Today because of the medical outposts, the iodine deficiency is no longer prevalent. I have never seen a cretin and Phurba does not know of any in the surrounding villages. Occasionally, a goiter can still be found but they are always in the elderly.

Sherpa parents take special precautions that they believe will assure the well-being of their children. If a baby cries all the time, the parents will change the baby's name. When taking a baby out at night, a black mark is put on the forehead and nose to keep the bad spirits away. It is believed that if children eat chicken hearts, they will be easily frightened individuals. If they eat pig, they will not speak when they grow up.

Babies are nursed until the third year of life. It might last longer but the mother usually has another baby by this time. The babies are strapped to the mothers' backs and taken into the fields. In the house they are placed in a basket. Frequently the basket is suspended from the rafters inside, or outside on a porch, so that the

Pemba's middle daughter playing with a basket typically used for hauling everything in the mountains. It is made from bamboo and is extremely tough, supporting loads of up to 150 pounds.

Nepalese child (not Sherpa) on Jugal Himal trek, baby-sitting younger sibling.

LORETTE WILMOT LIBRARY
NAZARETH COLLEGE

baby can swing. Toddlers are not given an afternoon nap as in America. They are expected to stay up all day and then they sleep from seven at night to six in the morning. In the winter babies are rarely bathed. In the unheated houses it makes sense. However, as soon as some warmth returns, water is heated for the babies.

I spent a delightful afternoon in Lukla watching two cousins, each with their two children under the age of four, heat water and bathe all four children one after another. There was much giggling and laughing. The mothers seemed to enjoy themselves as much as the children. The sun shone into the kitchen through large glass windows and remains in my mind illuminating an atmosphere of loving and caring.

In the summer, if they wear any clothing, the toddlers are given unique pants with no bottoms. In this way the mother does not have to be concerned with diapers.

Toys for children are limited. Our friend Pemba's three little girls had corn husk dolls and played with anything from the kitchen that their mother would let them take away. I have seen a few balls and wads of black rubber bands used like hacky sacks. On one trip we took back a frisbee for the boys. Like all children, they will invent something with which to play if there are no commercial toys available.

Winter in the Himalayas is truly a wonderland for the children. They put on all their clothes, though they rarely have coats since none are manufactured in this country, and go outside to frolic in the snow. Pieces of broken pottery water jars serve as sleds. What fantastic long runs they must have as they hop from field to field down through the village. The children do not make snowmen; they make gigantic balls of snow until they can no longer roll them. When the snow gets ten feet deep, as sometimes happens in the village, everyone stays inside. It might seem like a wonderful playground but without a firm crust it would be impossible to venture around and children could fall into the snow, unable to escape. The Sherpas do not seem to have thought of the idea of snowshoes.

Moving On

Formal training starts around seven or eight. Boys begin to carry water and learn the tasks of the farm. Girls help in the kitchen and take care of smaller children. It is common to see a seven- or eight-year-old with a baby strapped to her back. As the children grow, they help with waiting on guests in the house. In a land of no television there is a lot of visiting from house to house, especially

MAZARACONIBELL

in the months when little work can be done.

Boys go trekking at twelve, the age when they can get a government work permit. The money, of course, belongs to the family and the youngsters return home to work on the farm when there is no trekking.

Phurba's sister, Pasang Phuti, is two years younger than Phurba. At about the age of twenty she was unmarried and unable to get along with Mama anymore. She moved to Kathmandu and worked in a tea shop. I do not know whether she thought that she could find a husband there, but things did not work out. After three years in the city she arrived at our apartment, all teary-eyed, one morning to beg for money so that she could go back to the village. Of course, we sent her back. She was not long with Mama when she found a Sherpa carpenter to marry.

Sherpa women have as many children as they can. Often this means seven or eight. Mama had seven, a girl died at twelve and a boy at sixteen. Birth control pills are given at the Kunde hospital for free, but Kunde is a two-day walk away; besides, people are not interested in birth control. The children are wanted, just in case others die. They are much too valuable for work and taking care of the old.

Overpopulation is always a problem and Nepal, as mentioned previously, is one of the fastest-growing countries in terms of population (World Almanac 1992). It is not so much that there are people everywhere; there are vast stretches of land with no one inhabiting them—the mountains or the arid lands of western Nepal. However, arable land is what is important and only 17 percent of Nepal is arable (World Almanac 1992).

I saw an interesting program on TV about overpopulation. It actually compared a United States family of four and a Nepalese family of eight. The point of the program was that, in terms of harming the earth, the United States family far exceeded the Nepalese family, who produced no pollution, used nothing such as electricity (the production of which causes pollution), and threw nothing away (all garbage was either eaten by the animals or made into compost).

The Sherpa family has a lack of privacy. Most houses have only one room, so Sherpa children grow up knowing all about the facts of life. Teenagers are like teenagers the world over: they are interested in sex. Sherpas do not kiss romantically, and the parents take a dim view of premarital sex, but the teens manage it anyway. One good opportunity is when the teenagers guard the fields during the ripening of the crops. They live in chya khang in the fields. It is a simple matter for the youngsters to visit one another. If the parents find out about it, they will beat the youngsters. If a child is conceived, there is no abortion. The Sherpa belief in reincarnation negates abortion; hence abortions are very rare. A girl could go off to the hospital or Kathmandu for an abortion but her father must sign papers and they must pay for it. On the other hand, an illegitimate child makes the girl almost unmarriageable. Someone will eventually take her, but he will be a most socially undesirable mate.

Divorce is not a difficult or uncommon thing in Sherpa society. If both parties agree, then it is very simple. Sometimes the wife has no say—if she is unhappy, but if none of her relatives will take her in, she has no choice but to stay with the husband. Sometimes these women go off to Kathmandu.

It is another matter when a spouse dies. Frequently people remarry, especially if they are young and have no children. However, when it is an older person, his or her own children do not like to see a remarriage. Phurba's Mom was widowed at the age of forty-five. He does not want her to remarry, though he cannot give me any concrete reasons for this. I suspect it is because if she remarried and had another male child, then he would be the child who would inherit the house and half the land of the house; any additional male children will decrease the amount that each sibling inherits. On the other hand, her husband could have a farm and fields, but he might also have male children by a first marriage. If there would be such a marriage, it would make each sibling's share smaller.

Change is inevitable, even for the isolated Sherpa. Clothing and outward appearances are the first and easiest things to change. However, just because someone now wears bluejeans does not mean that that person has transformed on the inside. Beliefs are much harder to change than clothing.

6

Dying

Each society has its own unique way of dealing with death and dying, and almost every one must rely on religious principles to explain death and soften its blow. The Buddhists believe that those who leave this world early are simply to return to it in another form; a small, weak or handicapped baby will be reincarnated into a better life.

Deaths are frequent even in a small village of seventy adults, where maladies such as venereal diseases, scabies, amoebic dysentery, bacillary dysentery, fever, tuberculosis, pneumonia, bronchitis and gastroenteritis are common. One family in our village has had three babies die in the last five years. When children die, there is a very small ceremony and then the corpse is taken up to a high hill and set out for the birds to eat. Phurba's sister, Nang Lamu, died of measles at the age of twelve, and this is the type of funeral she received. Phurba's brother, Mingma Norbu, died at sixteen of white pustules in his mouth. When we got word of the death in the United States, my husband was naturally very upset. After a day's mourning he voiced a typical Buddhist philosophy. He said, "Dead is dead; gone is gone." That was the end of the mourning period.

After the death of an adult the lama pulls a few hairs out of the dead person's head, so the spirit may leave, and he chants a spell to help the spirit go. The horoscope is then cast to find the day for cremation. Much of what is done is because of fear of ghosts. Before the body is taken out of the house, four wood cutters leave the village to take the wood to the burning place.

Naphur (death ceremony) then takes place. When a baby dies, only the village people attend; the exception is the one lama who is summoned from a monastery. In the adult ceremony, two lamas are called to the house. One lama begins the ceremony before the body is removed by dancing in the house to ensure that the ghost will not come back and haunt the inhabitants. The lama's maroon robes billow out as he creates fantastic shadows on the walls. The yellow blouse and red sash contrast sharply and give him an incongruent carnival effect. As he dances he holds little finger cymbals in his left hand and a small drum with rappers suspended from string in his right hand. When he twirls the drum, the small rappers hit the drum head. Meanwhile, another lama blows on a human-thighbone flute.

Next, the body is stripped of its clothes and wrapped in a *chepar* (white cloth). The body has the Sipakhorlo (wheel of life) placed on its chest and is carried to the burning place, always up from the village. The men who carry the body have black marks on their cheeks and noses to drive ghosts away.

At the burning place the wood cutters hide when the body is brought close, because the highest ghost is waiting to eat the body and might take his revenge on the wood cutters, since he is robbed of the body by the fire. The pile of wood is about six-feet high and four-feet square and it angles up to a point. The body is placed, standing up, in the center of the wood pile. Rags soaked in kerosene have been placed on the ground with a rack over them to ensure good air flow. Some bodies burn in two hours, others take six to eight hours.

The lama dances around the body, as it begins to burn, to please the ghosts and ensure that the ghost of the person does not return. The dancing is very beautiful, dramatic and magical. The lama leaps into the air and twirls around, billowing out his robes—all the while chanting as the instruments echo in the mountains.

The night after the burning, at six or seven o'clock, the whole village gathers in the dead person's house to perform the Shayzum to make sure that the person does not come back to haunt the house. A boy of the village who has been born under the sign of the tiger carries a shield, which is really a bamboo-plaited tray. A funnel is placed on his head with a long string attached. In his other hand the boy carries the *kukuri* (traditional knife). The lama mixes black ink with butter and puts marks on the boy's forehead—one on each cheek, one on his chin and a long streak down his nose. Another person carries a bow that is made just for this ceremony. The boy kneels on his right knee with the kukuri pointing up and the shield protecting him. The man with the bow kneels behind the boy, so that the shield will protect him also. A thread cross is placed on the floor with a bowl of barley on top to attract and ensare the demons (Ortner 1978). The lama gives the signal to the people, and they begin to whistle and circle their right hands above their heads. The bow man is to shoot the ghost if it is seen. The people whistle three times and then get up and scream and walk all over the house. The lama then sculpts from dough a yak figurine with two people sitting on it. He makes two small flags with a magic charm written on them and puts one in the head of each dough man. A round dough receptacle is made and butter put inside with a wick for burning. These are taken to the closest crossroads. There the figurines are put down with the candle behind them. Then three stones are put on the ground with leaves on top. Behind the stones nine parallel lines are made across the trail with the kukuri. This will prevent the ghost from returning to the house.

After a week the people who carried the body to the burning place go to check the ashes. If they see the track of an animal, bird or man in the ashes, it means that the person will return in his next life as that animal or a man. These men then take the ashes and bury them, covering them with stones.

Meanwhile, a date is set for the next ceremony, Gyou Shaytu (rice giving and Scripture reading). It is usually scheduled about a month in advance, so that the word can get out to the surrounding villages and so that the people can arrange to come. The relative in charge of the Gyou Shaytu goes to the surrounding monasteries and contracts for lamas to attend. He gives them each 10 rupees to ensure that they do not go somewhere else on that day. The ceremony needs about fifteen lamas.

There are two parts to the ceremony. The Gyou is the rice-giving part and the Shaytu is when the lamas read the Scriptures. For days before the ceremony the family begins to prepare the food. Each person who comes must be given a ball of rice dough (approximately six inches in diameter and weighing about ten pounds). My father-in-law's Gyou Shaytu had between two hundred and three hundred people in attendance, including the children, making it very costly in terms of both the rice and the preparation time necessary. As in all Sherpa ceremonies, much rice was needed to make chang, since the chang must be made out of rice for special occasions.

The lamas arrive and begin to read the Shaytus. Each Shaytu takes one day to read. These Shaytus help to determine merit for the person and help with his next reincarnation. The number of Shaytus is determined by the money available. Each of the fifteen lamas is paid 55 rupees ($1.90) a day; in addition, each must be housed and fed. The average Nepalese makes $160 a year, so the $28.50 per day is very expensive. My husband had four Shaytus said for his father. Some families (who can afford it) have the lamas read for ten or fifteen days.

On the last day that the Shaytus are to be read, the people from all the surrounding villages arrive. Phurba sat on a table with his father's brother. On the table was a tray containing uncooked rice and a *khata* (white ceremonial cloth). One person stood by the table and constantly poured chang for everyone. Each family comes to the table, greets the relatives and puts whatever amount of money they can afford on the tray with the rice. Phurba received 4,000 rupees ($138). Everyone who comes receives a ball of rice dough, if the family can afford it; then each person also is given a ball of butter about three inches in diameter and 2 rupees can also be given. Our family could not afford the butter or money. Then everyone is served a big meal of rice, butter, noodles, meat and lots of chang.

The next morning the lamas are given all their rupees in a khata placed before them; another khata is placed around each lama's neck. The lamas then return to their monasteries.

The total cost of my father-in-law's Gyou Shaytu was approximately 21,000 rupees. Since Phurba received 4,000 rupees as gifts, the family had to provide $590. Phurba had to borrow the money from three or four different people to get enough. Three years later, after we were married, I finally paid off the debt. Phurba had been able to pay a little toward it; although there was some interest, it was low because all the money was borrowed within the village. One can imagine the suffering that these debts can cause. The earlier Naphur and Shayzum ceremonies also cost the family. A child's funeral is less expensive than an adult's, since a child under ten need only have the rice-giving ceremony and because it is confined to the village people.

The average life span in Nepal is 53.9 years for males and 51.1 years for females (World Almanac 1992). This is one of the few countries where the men outlive the women. In addition to the two older people in our village already mentioned in earlier chapters, about ten years ago there was another village woman who lived to be 100. Phurba's great-grandmother lived to be 125. She was one of the many Nepalese who had a goiter.

Many people in the village die in the spring. If the monsoon the year before has been too wet and many of the crops have rotted, the family will need a lot of money to buy food; those who do not have the money will go hungry. If a wet monsoon is coupled with hot May weather, with manure and flies everywhere, then it is little wonder that people get sick and die. On the other hand, the monsoon is looked upon as a positive regularity, a seasonal visitor that washes the land clean. For the Sherpa, life, too, has its seasons; being born carries with it the surety of dying.

7

Beliefs Make Reality

The Sherpas generally follow the Tibetan form of Buddhism, "believing in *sang-ngag* [the secret formulas] sub-sect of *nying-ma-pa*" (Kunwar 1989). However, they also have a generous helping of animism left over from some long forgotten past.

I will not pretend to be a Buddhist scholar. I have taught the basics in the classroom, but all the intricacies (and there are many) are not known to me. Phurba is no expert either. One day we compared the Ten Commandments with his beliefs and he agreed with all of them. Of course, he also believes in reincarnation.

Siddhartha Gautama was the son of a king of a small state in northern India. He was born in Lumbini in southern Nepal in 560 B.C. The borders between India and Nepal were rather vague at the time. Siddhartha became known as the Buddha, the Enlightened One, through his meditation and philosophy.

As many have stated before, Buddhism is more of a philosophy, a right path to follow, than it is a religion. Thus, a Sherpa is ingrained with kindness and generosity. No matter what house I went into in the village, I was met with the most wonderful courteous manner. Sherpas are exceptional hosts. We were always pressed with food and drink. At parties the guests were never allowed to leave until everything was eaten and all the chang or arak was drunk.

Fate is tied up centrally in everything to a Buddhist. Peaceful attitudes have always been associated with Buddhists. My husband worries about nothing; everything has been preordained. Things will happen when and how they are supposed to happen.

On the outside Sherpas have a very peaceful, loving, joyful veneer, totally in keeping with Buddhist teachings. But not all is

61

sanguine. Sometimes, especially when drunk, that peacefulness explodes. I have seen several domestic fights occur when both parties were drunk. One evening in the village Pasang Rinzee, a man from across the river asked Phurba how much money we had and they nearly came to blows. Both men were very drunk. The women actually sat on Phurba to stop him from fighting the older Pasang. It was an awful gaffe that Pasang had made and the village talked about it for days to follow. Similar fighting occurs when the men go to Kathmandu. If the men do not find work, then boredom gives way to drinking and fights ensue.

The villagers follow the basic beliefs of Buddhism and they leave the rest to the lamas. There is the village lama who performs the small, everyday ceremonies. He has his own books. They are in Tibetan script, loose leaf, bound by boards and tied with ribbons. They have beautiful illuminations on some of the pages. Our village has no monastery; the closest one is in lower Lukla, about one-and-a-half hours' walk away. Thangboche, two days north, is the leading monastery of the area, even though it was one of the last monasteries to be founded in this region, in about 1916. It is known throughout the world. Pangboche and Thame Monasteries seem to be the first founded in the later half of the seventeenth Century (Ortner 1989). One hour north of Thangboche is Devuche, a nunnery. Another nunnery is located at Bigu, several days walk to the south from Bhuwa/Shurkey.

The Buddhists clang bells and cymbals and drums to attract the gods. They burn juniper to please them. Their holy scriptures have 108 books and their prayer beads have 108 beads. The wooden prayer wheels are carved with the words of prayers, and inside each wheel is a piece of paper with more prayers written on it. The prayers are sped to heaven when the wheel is twirled in a clockwise direction. The rotation of the prayer wheels achieves merit, so people always spin them as they pass by them. The design of the prayer wheels varies. Some are hand held and others are as large as ten feet; some are plain wood, others are gaily painted.

Monasteries and rich Buddhists decorate their walls with lavish paintings. They are outstandingly beautiful, colorful and, to my Western eyes, sometimes scary. Since most of the monasteries have few windows and poor lighting, it is a mystical and frightening experience to view the paintings. As a flashlight delves into the far corners, fantastic figures appear as if from midair. Panning with the light, more bizarre shapes emerge. Each tells a story that is to guide the Buddhist's life.

I have been in some houses that are decorated with these paintings, but there are none in our poor village; only the village lama has a few small pictures. There are no *thangkas* (wheels of

These are the village mani stones, the only monument in the village of Shurkey. The stone path on the left leads to Lukla, a one-hour walk away. Pemba and Kami's lodge is on the hill on the right.

life), *mani* walls (walls of rock that have prayers carved into them), *chhungyar* (prayer wheels—small or large water-powered ones), or *gondas* (temples, monasteries) in our village. Likewise, *Kani* (a village entry gate) and *chorten* (a monument with a domed roof) do not exist. We do have one small grouping of mani stones, as well as hand-held prayer wheels and some prayer flags. Mama has a pole, but the flag has long since disappeared. Phurba helped Pasang Rinzee put up a new prayer flag one warm, clear February day. The flag is six inches wide and 20 feet long, printed with black ink prayers taken from old wooden blocks. Phurba helped Kami erect two prayer flags when his new house/lodge was finally completed.

Pasang Rinzee has often stated that he wanted to build a gonda on a high, rocky hill at the south end of the village. The rest of the villagers scoff at him. Where would he ever get enough money for a gonda? He does have three large, costly clay Buddhas and an altar in his father's house, which he owns since his father is dead.

Torma are sacrificial cakes for the gods. People use them instead of sacrificing animals, which would be too costly. Mama puts little mounds of flour on the edge of teacups and chang cups

The men are helping to put up Kami's new prayer flag; they are levering the pole into a three-foot hole dug earlier. The pole must have been cut from Kami's forest land. The prayer flags along the storage shed were being strung for the New Year's celebration. Kami needed this additional shed since most of his house is a trekking lodge.

as an offering to the gods. People can perform their own small ceremonies, but complex ones require lamas.

There are two basic types of lamas in the monasteries. The *seta* teach and the *dupda* perform rituals. All monasteries try to find a reincarnated head lama. When the head lama dies, they search for a child of three or four who can recognize the former lama's possessions, clothing, rooms, and so forth. In the Khumbu there is a reincarnated lama at Thangboche, the leading monastery of the Khumbu, and one at Thame. The Solu has at least one at Lamobagar. The head lama is all things: healer of misfortune, teacher, medical man, prophet, fortune teller and ritual expert.

The monasteries have many rooms, as the lamas live and work there as well as worship. The worship room contains at least one altar. On it are several shelves. On the first shelf are eight basic offerings: water for drinking and water for washing, a flower for good smell, burnt incense, butter for fire or a butter lamp, scented water, simple uncoated torma and an instrument symbolizing music. The second shelf has offerings representing the senses: a mirror for the eyes, an instrument which produces sound for the ears, incense for the nose, food for taste, and cloth for touch. The third shelf has sacrificial cakes and butter lamps. Other things found on the shelves are items such as food, a scepter (a symbol of wisdom), a bell, a sacred wand adorned with silk streamers in five colors, a holy jug with peacock feathers, a thighbone trumpet, a conch shell which is blown during ceremonies, cymbals, tea and a drum. A life is believed to be recorded by the god of death using white and black pebbles, which are heaped upon the shoulders. On death the horrible spirit that controls the wheel of life weighs the pebbles and assigns the next life.

Sherpas carry their destiny on their foreheads. Therefore, Sherpas do not like anyone touching their heads—their *sonam* (merit) must not be harmed. However, if this occurs, they can repair any damage to their sonam by gift giving to the lamas; hospitality; circumambulating a gonda, chorten or mani wall; prayers; printing prayer flags; building bridges, mani walls or gondas; carving mani stones; or having religious paintings made.

Giving alms is also a part of Buddhism. Even though my husband had practically nothing when I met him, he still gave a few pennies to an old Sherpa woman begging in Kathmandu at Swayambhu Monastery. It is also the old who are seen with the prayer wheels and prayer beads; they are storing merit for their future life.

The main prayer of the Buddhist religion begins, "*Om Mani Padme Hum*"; it means "The jewel is in the lotus" and comes from an old tale from the time of creation. Phurba often mutters this under his breath.

As mentioned in chapter 3, Buddhists are absolutely not allowed to kill anything. When I first brought Phurba to the United States, he would not even kill a fly; he would merely catch them and put them outside. Maybe I have corrupted him because he does kill insects now, but he sees no need to crawl up into the corner of the ceiling to kill a spider. I have become the mass murderer of our family.

Some mountains are considered the dwelling places of gods and therefore are sacred. The Hindu Nepalese government has gone along with this and has therefore made some places off-limits to climbers. The Buddhists believe that some of these mountains are considered female deities, and some lakes are also looked on as the repositories of spirits.

Consulting the Dhadur

The Sherpa practice of animism, the belief in spirit beings, is left over from the days before Buddhism. The Sherpa, like many other peoples, have integrated animism into their own religion. Before any event, the people want to know the auspicious days, so they consult the Dhadur (The Tibetan book of dates)—they go to the village lama who reads out of this ancient book. Additionally, the first fifteen days of the month are considered auspicious and the eighth, tenth, fifteenth and twenty-ninth are considered sacred.

Sherpas see spirits everywhere. The doors to all Sherpa houses are low so that the stiff-backed spirits, the *hrendi*, cannot easily enter. These are spirits that were never human, and they wander and cause harm to people. There are other spirits called *pem*. They are like light and are the mind of a person who is sleeping. When everyone in the house is asleep the pem can wander about. Often six or seven pem come together and try to make the people sick. Also, if a pem is caught under a basket, then the person to whom it is attached will become sick. Still other spirits are called *tatok*, spirits of the dark. When a person, who is alone in the dark, gets scared, it is probably because of a tatok; the person will probably fall sick.

One day, on the trek where I met my husband, our trekking group came upon a soothsayer, *lhawa minung*, sitting near a house. Someone in the house was sick and the lhawa minung was communicating with the dead and asking them to stop making the person sick. The lhawa minung was seated outside behind a bench that was covered in white cloth. On the bench were nine silver bowls, each containing water, rice, oil or butter. He was burning incense, twirling a drum, ringing a bell and chanting. Lhawa minung are often employed to attempt to control spirits.

Dreams are thought to be spirits influencing the person's mind. If a person dreams of a girl riding a white horse, that is a very bad omen for the girl. If the dream is that someone's house has fallen down, that means bad luck. If there is a dream that someone dies, then the person dreamed about will probably do so.

Phurba has seen spirits twice, when he was only ten or so. Both times he was at Pasang Rinzee's bridge in the village and both times were around dusk. In the first instance a man started coming after Phurba. He screamed and the spirit disappeared. The second time there were two well-dressed women near the bridge, but when they turned around they were naked.

Other Sherpa beliefs are revealed in their daily habits. I am not allowed to leave my shoes on the floor soles up; that is very inauspicious. Nor should I point the soles of my feet at someone for I could be accused of wishing them bad luck. Each time we have left the village, the village lama has had to be present at our departure to ensure a safe journey, especially since we were to walk through the forest where many spirits reside. He makes us drink some chang and chants as we say goodbye to the family. As we usually leave in the early morning, the chang is a real eye-opener.

Happy Losar

Sherpa festivals are a combination of religion and magic. Losar, the New Year, is in February; its precise date depends on the moon. In preparation for Losar, the Sherpa put up new decorations in their houses. To make the decorations they mix flour, water and a little butter together to form a paste. This paste is used to adorn cabinets and wooden walls with words and drawings of such things as pots, chickens, *chortens*, and so forth. Brother Mingma, who did all the decorating the New Year I was in the village, wrote "Happy New Year" (in English) on one of the cabinet doors. Only "Hap" was on one line, "pyne" on the next, and "wyer" on the third. He also painted "Well" on one line and "come to" on the next and "Sherpa" on the third, with "Good Luck" underneath. The New Year is the time of cleaning and new clothes. Several villagers give New Year's parties in the week or so of the celebration. In our village the village lama gave the first party, ours was the second, and Kami and Pemba had the third. There was much feasting, drinking, laughing, joking, singing and dancing. The people went home only when the chang and arak ran out.

Several days before the party at our house, the brothers made arak/rakshi. Before our party began the village lama arrived. Containers of arak and chang were set before him. Phurba put three triangular pieces of butter representing sitting Buddhas, on the edge of the pail. A plate with three lumps of butter (on the edge) and some corn and rice was put before the lama. Mama also put some of the corn and rice in the chang, and Phurba sprinkled a small amount of salt and flour on top. The lama was given a cup of arak with the flour blessing. He drank it. Rhododendron leaves and sprigs of juniper were set on fire in front of the lama. Then the lama took a peacock feather and began to chant. He flicked the end of the feather in the chang and sprinkled it about. Then he took the rice and threw it around the room. The family seemed to ignore what was going on, continuing their chores, but when the proper time came they all joined in with the chanting. The lama drank some more chang. His voice was deep and resonant, echoing in his chest cavity.

The entire village of seventy adults and many children came for a meal at our house that day. Villagers often vent their frustrations with one another at these gatherings through rather vicious joking and reciprocal joking. It appears that joking takes place in the social context, so the jokers can see what village support they might have. Joking sometimes leads to threatening arguments or near violence. As violence is about to erupt the meal is served; this diversion calms everyone. In the evening singing and dancing take place. Our village has no instruments so the music consisted entirely of singing, which sounded more like chanting. When they danced they formed a line around the room and put their arms around each other's waists. I quickly found out that each song had its own set of intricate steps which everyone knew except me. There was much stomping of feet and swaying back and forth. It was a wonderful evening listening to the songs and watching the dancers.

At the last party at Pemba and Kami's, when we were reaching the bottom of the barrel of arak, the lama went around and blessed everyone. With the help of two other men, he placed flour in a circle around our shoulders and mouths. Then we had to drink a teacup of arak straight down. The amount of arak in the cup and how much flour you received depended on how much the men had had to drink. Some people were nearly covered with flour from head to toe. This blessing would ensure good luck for the coming year.

Tsah takes place in October and is the equivalent of our Thanksgiving. Two or three people, called *tsah lhawa*, give torma (dough sacrifice), and then two or three commit themselves for the torma for next year. This brings them merit. The village lama performs a two-and-a-half hour ceremony and then the people eat. There is much feasting, as the crops are all in from the fields, and so there is a great variety of food available.

Lupsang is a personal ceremony for the house and can be done on any "good day." The village lama does his ceremony and the people drink chang.

Yungnay occurs in November or December and it lasts for three or four days. It is very expensive and usually two or three people have to share the cost. The Sherpa participating in this event earn merit by praying and fasting and do not speak for the time period. Everyone else comes at the end of the fasting and the people who have done the Yungnay must provide rice, yogurt, butter, vegetables, potatoes, meat and tsampa. If word of this gets past the village, then the people from all around come, which makes it more expensive for the participants.

Phurba and Donna with flour blessing at Pemba and Kami's New Year's celebration. The flour, administered by the village lama, invokes good luck in the coming year. Each person then had to drink a cup of arak (grain alcohol).

Mani-Rimdu is celebrated in the Khumbu. It is held at Thangboche Monastery in November or early December and at Thame Monastery in May. It is a dance festival where lamas dress up as certain spirits and act out the traditional stories. There is a National Geographic video, "Return to Everest" (1984), that shows this ceremony at Thame Monastery. Hillary is there, as is Phurba's aunt from the nearby village of Nakbug/Mushay (she is the beautiful Sherpa woman sitting right in front of Hillary).

Dumje, a general celebration for the blessing of the village, is not practiced in our village. Phurba says that sometimes our villagers go to a local monastery at Ghumela and celebrate, though he has never done so. According to those who have participated in Dumje, there is dancing all night and all food is bought at food stalls set up by the Sherpa.

As is commonly known, animism is tied very closely with nature worship. Buddhists are very much "nature people" with their philosophy about fire, water, wind, and so forth. The course of nature greatly affects the Sherpas. Earthquakes are believed to be caused by small, furry creatures who live underground. When the creature wiggles its ears it causes earthquakes. Eclipses are much feared. The Sherpa women tend to scream a lot during an eclipse, while some men blow horns made out of cow horns. Many people twirl prayer wheels, recite prayers and light butter candles. The less religious look for stones with ants' nests under them. They believe that when they take the stones away, the noise of the ants goes up into the sky and helps the sun or moon to return.

Religion still has a very strong hold on the Sherpas. Buddhism with animism encompasses everything that the people do. From birth to death the Sherpas are guided by the spirits along a path that is foreordained for them. When people's lives are excessively hard, they look ahead and hope that their next life will be better.

8

The Order of Life

Sherpa society is not as concerned with social status as are many other societies; however, within the village there is still some distinction between people. For example, there are several families who are poorer than the rest, but there is no family that is fabulously wealthy.

Sherpas have been fortunate throughout their history, since most families have always owned their own land. When the first Sherpas arrived in the Khumbu, it was an empty area, which they merely had to settle. There is no one in our village, or even in the surrounding villages, who does not own at least a small field, and many families own fields in more than one village. Some even own plots in distant villages. Because it would be nearly impossible for them to make the journeys required to keep the crops, they use a system similar to sharecropping. In the Sherpa system of share-cropping, the man who owns the field supplies all the seed to the man who agrees to farm the field; then they split the crop in equal parts. Sometimes these extra fields are just rented for money, but the farmer who takes the additional field always has a farm of his own.

Mama's next-door neighbor had been the wealthiest man in the village. He had many, many zum which supplied much milk and butter. He had one son, one daughter who had a disability and so never married, and one daughter who married and subsequently died. He eventually sold his zum for a large amount of money. One day a non-Sherpa from the Solu came to visit the man. The visitor had actually built this man's house and many other houses in the area. The visitor asked our neighbor for quite a substantial loan, which he was given along with a written paper stating the loan and

71

the amount of interest. When the time came for the first payment nothing was heard of the man. Our neighbor found out that this man also borrowed from other people. The people who were owed money went to the debtor's house in the Solu, but his wife and children said that he was now staying in Kathmandu. The people did not go that far after him. They did not consult the police, even though they had papers proving that the man owed them money. There is a feeling toward the police in the Sherpa society—not exactly fear, more like abhorrence perhaps. A Kathmandu lawyer-friend has explained that in Nepal when a case is taken to court, the courts are very slow to proceed and oftentimes nothing happens. If opponents cannot mediate a problem, it might as well be forgotten.

Pasang Rinzee, from across the river, is now the wealthiest man in the village. Pasang Rinzee, a man who is now about fifty, had done much expedition work in his youth; he even once traveled to Italy. His family had already been in good standing so he merely added to a good beginning. Pasang Rinzee owns many fields and used to own two houses. He has since sold his own house to a trekking agency that was setting up a system of lodges along the trail to Everest. Most trekking agencies take tents but the "new" method is to have lodges. I have spent many afternoons and evenings in Pasang Rinzee's kitchen watching his wife, Kanti, cook. Kanti's brother, Lhakpa, has married Elaine Brook, a well-known British outdoor writer. Pasang Rinzee, Kanti, their four children, and Pasang Rinzee's aged mother have moved across the village now into Pasang Rinzee's father's house. Pasang Rinzee's mother, Pha Nima, has always taken a particular interest in me. Being taller than most Sherpas and with blond hair and blue eyes, I was a real curiosity to these people. Pha Nima would take my hand whenever we met and continue to hold it not leaving my side until we left. I had difficulty eating at one New Year's party until someone convinced Pha Nima that I really needed two hands to eat. Unfortunately, Pasang Rinzee is suffering with what I believe to be serious ulcers. He has great difficulty doing any work.

Kami and Pemba seem to be the up-and-coming young couple in our village. Both in their twenties, they are energetic workers. Kami seeks expedition work, which pays the most. His father is the village lama, which may increase his intrinsic social status but not his monetary position. Pemba is such a hard worker. She farms, runs the lodge and cooks a lot for the villagers. Hers is one of the traditional nightly meeting spots. Frequently I have seen villagers drinking chang at Kami and Pemba's house but not having to pay for it.

Other villages, such as Nauche/Namche Bazaar and Khumjung have wealthier people. The Nauche/Namche Bazaar wealth is some-

*Pasang Rinzee, his wife Kanti and her niece, who was living and working
with them.*

what old, being derived from earlier trading with Tibet. Today
Nauche/Namche Bazaar, Khumjung, and Khunde receive most of
their new wealth from expeditions.

One way that Sherpas do make money is through loans, called
kheen. If you borrow a small amount of money ($20, for example)
and pay it back in two or three months, then no interest is charged.
If a larger amount of money is borrowed, but still not a great amount
($50 perhaps) and you pay it back in a year, then a small amount
of interest is charged. If an even larger amount is borrowed
(approximately $100 or more), then a written document is drawn
up, witnessed and as much as 40 percent interest is charged.
Usually people incur these debts due to death. As an alternative,
some people, if they have valuable jewelry, will pawn it when they
need money and get the jewelry back when they can.

Make Room by the Fire

Jewelry is one way of telling social rank. Almost all Sherpa
women have gold earrings. If they do not, then it indicates how poor
they are. A kyetee, large silver belt buckle, some eight-inches long
by four-inches wide and embossed all over, is quite expensive.
Pemba has one. While I was in the village the women were showing
around a necklace with large pieces of turquoise and orange coral

A noon meal in Pasang Rinzee's kitchen. Pha Nima, his mother, is second from the left about to drink chang (which is white in color). All the glasses are filled with chang, the plates are piled with rice, and the bowls contain a mixture of vegetables and a small portion of meat. Mama is third from the left. All the houses have collections of pictures of family members on the walls, as seen here.

beads. It cost somewhere around $150, practically a full year's wages. Like the American Indians and the Tibetans, the Sherpas value turquoise very highly.

Generally, one can determine the wealth of the family by animals, copper pots and jewelry. Those who own trekking companies in Kathmandu are especially admired. Of course, if the company is successful, then they can be very wealthy. Our friend, Lhakpa Sonam, and his wife, Pasang, have all the modern conveniences, including servants. Pasang is from our village and naturally everyone knows how successful she and Lhakpa Sonam are and how lucky her family is. Luck seems to mean more than social status; perhaps it even *is* social status.

The Sherpas are gracious hosts. People take positions on the benches or floor according to their status. Thus, the village lama was always given the seat next to the fire. Once, when we flew into Lukla, we brought a good deal of items from Kathmandu: food,

Mama is looking out of her kitchen window. When guests arrive they talk into the window until someone hears them and invites them in; no one ever knocks on a door. The doorway to the stable below the window is very low in order to prevent spirits from entering the house, and there is a good-luck charm on the doorframe. The stones of the house have been plastered with red clay.

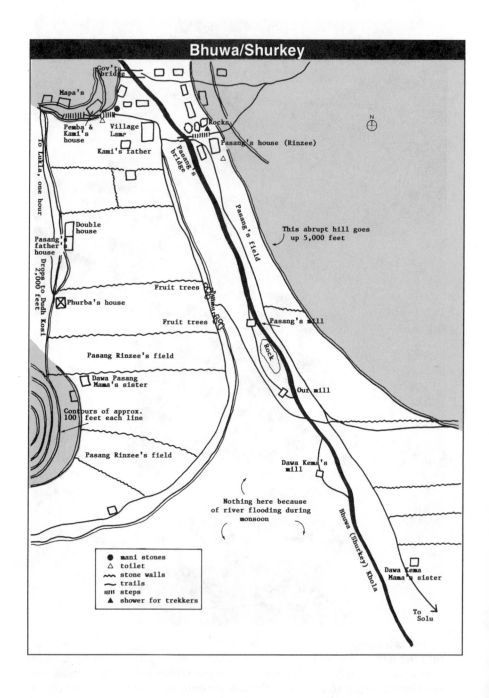

Bhuwa/Shurkey

Gov't bridge
Mapa's
Pemba & Kami's house
Village Lama
Kami's father
Rocks
Pasang's house (Rinzee)
Pasang's bridge
To Lukla, one hour
Double house
Pasang's father's house
Drops to Dudh Kosl 2,000 feet
Fruit trees
Phurba's house
Fruit trees
Pasang Rinzee's field
Dawa Pasang Mama's sister
Contours of approx. 100 feet each line
Pasang Rinzee's field
Pasang's field
This abrupt hill goes up 5,000 feet
Pasang's mill
Rock
Our mill
Dawa Kema's mill
Nothing here because of river flooding during monsoon
Bhuwa (Shurkey) Khola
Dawa Kema Mama's sister
To Solu

● mani stones
△ toilet
⌇ stone walls
— trails
⁞⁞⁞⁞ steps
▲ shower for trekkers

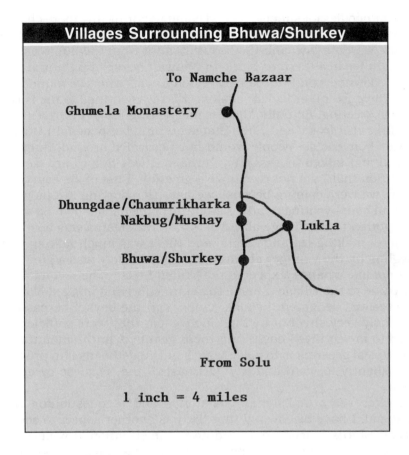

clothes and other things for the family. We could not carry
everything ourselves so we asked to hire someone. The only person
available and willing to porter for us was an elderly gentleman who
appeared to be seventy, at least. Phurba did not know him. When
we arrived at Mama's, he took the seat at the far end of the bench.
Mama fed him potatoes, tea, and chang; this was not part of the
prearranged pay. Although he was not a center of attention, he did
enter the conversation from time to time, and after he was
sufficiently rested he slipped quietly out the door.

When people want to enter a house, they do not knock on the
door. Since Mama's house has no glass in the windows, they quietly
call out until Mama comes to the window and invites them in. If
the house has glass in the windows, usually a door is left standing
open and the people call out there before entering.

I was always treated with extreme courtesy. When I could not
eat the food, because of the chilis mostly, Pemba would make me

instant noodles for supper. When I could not drink any more chang, Kanti would make me instant coffee (!). All the relatives called me Baaju, sister-in-law, and the beautiful aunt from Nakbug/Mushay brought tea in a thermos bottle to Bhuwa/Shurkey for Phurba and me. Everyone said Phurba had "Good Luck" when he found me.

One custom, or lack of custom, that was strange to me is the village greeting. Actually, there is no greeting. Upon Phurba's and my first visit from the United States nothing happened. In United States households, people would have crowded around, hugged, kissed and talked incessantly. Perhaps it was due to my lack of attention that I did not recognize a greeting. First of all, everyone knew we were coming because we had been staying in Lukla for several hours visiting relatives after the plane had landed. So word had gotten to the village ahead of our arrival. Mama was bustling around, making tea and chang, and there was much talking and giggling by the younger children. So I guess there was a greeting but not like what we expect in the United States. The second time we came to the village, I made the extra effort and hugged Mama, she seemed delighted. I shook hands with the boys. Sherpas are normally very shy, but by the time we left, they were sufficiently used to me so that I could hug them goodbye. In the mountains the typical greeting is to place your hands together as if in prayer, bow slightly forward and say "Namaste," the Nepalese greeting word.

After years of listening to stories and of questioning my husband, I have discovered that there is another aspect to social status. Status is accrued according to the elevation at which one lives—with higher status being assigned to those at higher altitudes. My questions about certain people often resulted in the answer, "He's from lower down." When I prodded further I was told that the ones lower down are not as well off as those at higher altitudes. In wealth? Well, yes but . . . Those who live at higher elevations, say at Nauche/Namche Bazaar or Khumjung, are much better positioned according to Sherpa belief. It seems to be linked with the ability to do the high-elevation climbing expeditions with greater ease and therefore the ability to receive more jobs. So it is money: more jobs, more money. My husband's village situated at 7,700 feet, is middle class in these terms. They are much better off in terms of status than are those of lower elevations, but do not do as well as those of the higher villages. This status difference strikes me as odd, because those of the lower elevations are often better nourished since they can grow more crops in the tropical climate. Those families of the higher elevations are not as fortunate, in my terms, since little grows at elevations of 12,000 feet and up. They must spend more money for food, and they must pay for any wood for building, which they then must carry up to the higher elevations, which are above the tree line.

Social rank becomes more distinct with those of other ethnic groups. The Sherpas view themselves as the best people. All the lowlanders are inferior. When in Kathmandu, Sherpas socialize mostly with Sherpas. Almost all the people in the trekking companies are Sherpas. If they need a place to stay or food to eat and they have no money, they go to relatives or to a Sherpa house. They stick together like glue. Phurba knows all the Sherpa people in the Khumbu and many in the Solu. There are other pockets of Sherpa settlements but he does not know the people from the Langtang, Manang, and such areas, unless he has met them trekking.

There are many different ethnic groups in Nepal. The Sherpas do not view these groups equally; some are considered untouchable, either for their group of origin or for their occupation, such as the *kami* (blacksmiths) and the people whom Phurba calls Khamandu, Yuckpa and Jirels. Jirels actually speak Sherpa but Sherpas will not invite them into their houses.

Sherpas are not supposed to marry people from other ethnic groups, but some do. It does not seem as if the Sherpas become greatly upset with the intermarriages; however, most of these people take up residence in Kathmandu. While there are occasional visitors, there are no non-Sherpas living in our village.

I tried to plot a family tree but it becomes very confusing. Phurba cannot remember back too far, and people are frequently divorced, or the spouse has died and they have taken another. Phurba has four brothers and two sisters. His mother has three sisters, one of whom is living in Darjeeling, India, and two brothers, but one is a step-brother since Mama's father died and her mother remarried. Phurba's father, who had died before I met Phurba, had no full-blooded sisters or brothers. Phurba's paternal grandmother died after Phurba's father was born. Phurba's father had three step-sisters and two step-brothers. Further back than this Phurba's stories start to get a bit vague. (He does know that his father's grandmother lived to be 125 years old.) Also, various terms do not seem to coincide. Phurba names many people uncle, aunt and cousin, but when I ask specifically who they are he cannot tell me or I find that they are cousins of very distant relation.

The Sherpa families usually include patrilineal extended family. Since the youngest son inherits the farmhouse and half of the farm's fields, it is then his responsibility to take care of the parents. In this manner the older sons can build up some wealth before they have to move out on their own. Meanwhile, they help to care for their younger brothers and sisters. The father is supposed to build a house for the eldest son, usually on the other half of the original farm. Other sons then move to fields that the family owns in that village or other villages. If there are too many sons or not enough fields, then a middle son or two will be sent off to the monastery. Today many of these sons are avoiding this by moving to Kathmandu. Most families have older members living with them. Aunts and uncles do sometimes live with nieces and nephews— mainly when they have had no children (rarely) or when their children have died. There are great feelings of responsibility toward older members of the family and helping any family member who is in trouble. Sherpas will always think of their family members first in any dealings whether trade, jobs and so on, then those of their village come next, followed by those of surrounding villages.

The older members of the society have positive social status. They are the historians, since Sherpa is an unwritten language. They remember past situations that are similar to present ones and are consulted for advice. They receive places of honor in the houses. When there are gatherings, such as parties, the first to be served is always the leading male of the house, then the village lama and then the oldest to the youngest in descending order, males first and then females.

Respect is a key word when thinking of social status among the Sherpas. It is those who have gained experience, the elders, who have the most respect. Though Sherpas are not as bound to male-female differentiation as some peoples are, there is still an idea that males are the superior.

There is still another factor that generates social status: government recognition. From early days the government in Kathmandu appointed Sherpas as *pembu* (tax collectors) in the Solu Khumbu. The reasoning seemed to be that the highly independent Sherpas would respond better to tax payments collected by one of their own. Also, the lowlanders were Hindu which might have caused antagonism among the Buddhists if the Hindus were placed in this position. Today the pembu also assumes the title and the duties of the *phurdon puntza* (village headman). He is elected by the villagers over whom he governs and therefore gains social status through his selection for this government post and through the money gained legally or illegally. The phurdon puntza works alongside his assistants, several local Sherpa people and one non-Sherpa from the central government. When I last visited the village, our phurdon puntza was not in Bhuwa/Shurkey. Rather, he was by the trails, northwest in Dhungdae/Chaumrikharka (meaning *zum* place), a trek that goes through Nakbug/Mushay. Our headman's area extends from Bhuwa/Shurkey in the south to

Thumbug/Jorsale in the north (which is just south of Nauche/Namche Bazaar), a distance of ten miles through the northern end of the Pharak valley. Since the change of government in 1990, this particular man has been voted out of power.

Of course, the phurdon puntza's first duty is tax collection. He sends his non-Sherpa assistant to the villages to announce that it is tax time and that the people are to go to the headman's house to pay their taxes. The non-Sherpa assistant is chosen because the Sherpas take more seriously a man from Kathmandu rather than someone local; also, if there is animosity about taxes, that anger can be directed to the non-Sherpa, allowing the local officials to maintain their social stature.

The phurdon puntza's second duty is to serve as the link between the villager and the government in Kathmandu. The villagers can petition the phurdon puntza for things the village needs, such as bridges. The phurdon puntza then presents the case to the central government and, if approved, the phurdon puntza becomes the coordinator of the project.

Thirdly, the village phurdon puntza is an arbitrator of disputes. If there is a disagreement between families or villages, it is his responsibility to see that it is worked out, and he has the ability to hand out fines. If the quarrel turns to violence, the phurdon puntza then calls in the Nepalese police. It does not appear that there are serious crimes in the Khumbu. Such things as robbery do not exist. There are few people who have more possessions than others, and it is not the Buddhist way to covet a neighbor's possessions—many times neighbors will give or share what they have with others. Early in my relationship with Phurba I had problems with him keeping anything I had given him. Invariably, watches, sunglasses (those are the two really big status symbols it seems), sweaters, jackets, and such, would end up with anyone who expressed a desire for them, especially his brothers. I have never heard of a murder in our area—at least one has never been reported—however, there are stories of people being poisoned about which the police are not told.

Once every five years the phurdon puntza sells such items as salt and rice to all the people of his village at half-price. These products are allotted according to number of family members. Also, if there is ever a very poor family who cannot afford to buy rice for a funeral, he then sells them the rice for half-price. As this brief description reveals, a village headman has many duties and needs to know his constituency well.

When Education Is Secondary

Education in the Khumbu is a project on which Hillary has worked for years. Without him there probably would not be any schools in the area. The first school he built was at Khumjung in 1961. My husband's school at Dhungdae/Chaumrikharka is a three-hours' walk, one way (for a child). All the children from the surrounding villages come to the school. Lukla, a rather large community by Sherpa standards, has a school but only for the first two grades. After that the children must walk the two hours to Dhungdae/Chaumrikharka. The video "Return to Everest" (1984) features this school and the construction of others.

The Nepalese government has only three years of compulsory education. Because the schools are often so far away, the children do not attend regularly. Children are to begin their schooling by seven, but a four-hour walk is quite a distance to travel everyday. Sometimes there are relatives who live close to the school and the children stay there for a few days, but the childrens' families cannot depend on these people all the time. January is the month that the schools have off because of the bad weather. However, the monsoon months can make the trails just as difficult to travel with slippery mud and wiggling leeches on every leaf. There are also certain times of the year when the children are needed for farm work; education is then secondary. It took my husband six years to complete his three years of compulsory education.

The Nepalese literacy rate is 29 percent (World Almanac 1992). I was surprised to learn that my mother-in-law could not read or write. Phurba just took it for granted that I knew that Sherpa girls did not go to school. Even today there are few girls in the Sherpa schools. The students are taught to read and write Nepalese (Sherpa is an unwritten language) and to do basic math. There is no history, geography, health or anything about the outside world until one reaches the upper grades, which many Sherpas do not. It is also a shame that most of the classes are taught in Nepalese by non-Sherpas. I would like Sherpa culture to be kept alive through the schools.

The school at Dhungdae/Chaumrikharka goes to the seventh-grade level. The children must go to Khumjung for grades eight, nine, and ten. Khumjung is a day-and-a-half travel north of Bhuwa/Shurkey. That means that the students from our village must live with someone. We do not seem to have any relatives in Khumjung, so if our brother, Lhakpa Gelu, wants to go to school there we will have to pay for him to live with someone and we will have to make arrangements for his board. It is not a simple matter to obtain his meals. We cannot buy food, so we will have to bring it to him from our farm. This also means that Lhakpa Gelu's labor will be missed at our farm. In really critical periods of farm labor, Lhakpa Gelu will probably go home for a week or two to help. As I write he is in the seventh level and the star pupil of the school at Duhngdae/Chaumrikharka, so we will soon have to make a decision on what he will do when he reaches the eighth grade. Lhakpa Gelu was supposed to become a monk, but, when Phurba left home for the United States, the family only had three sons in Bhuwa/Shurkey and they felt that it would be safer to have Lhakpa Gelu at home. Brother Nha Temba, who is now eleven, does not go to school. Cute, darling little Nha Temba must stay home to care for the cows. I try to encourage them to send him to school, but, at a distance of 12,000 miles, my arguments do not mean much. The cows are of immediate importance, whereas education does not seem to be so urgent. The last letter we received now tells us that Nha Temba has been sent to the monastery.

If a child wants to go to college, he or she must be sent to Kathmandu. That again means paying for the education as well as for food and board. We have relatives in Kathmandu so it would not be a problem for our family. There are elementary and high school boarding schools in Kathmandu, but they are very expensive. Pasang Rinzee's oldest son attended boarding school in Kathmandu, but he was the only child from our village doing so in 1990.

It is very hard to convince people who are fatalistic that there is worth in education. The Sherpa prefer to stay in the villages or go on expeditions and try to ignore everything else. What brings a family social status and merit is sending one of their sons to a monastery to become a lama. Since the oldest son is expected to work for the family while the rest of the children are young and since the youngest son is expected to care for the parents, one of the middle sons is usually sent. However, few children want to make the material sacrifices necessary to become a lama—especially with the encroachment of Western influences. Boys are typically sent at the age of eight or so to start their training. Imagine what a young child experiences upon seeing his older brothers with wrist watches, sunglasses, blue jeans and maybe a radio, and all the while wishing that he could have the same. If the family insists, he will have to go to the monastery, but fewer families are insisting these days.

As described above, in the older days social status was tied tightly with the Sherpas' Buddhist philosophy. Today it has a much looser association. As Western civilization encroaches, it becomes more important to the Sherpa to own Western articles. Therefore, social status becomes influenced by the ability to obtain Western goods. Those who can go on expeditions and obtain these objects have increased status over those who cannot. One thing the Sherpa have not imported from Westerners is their belief in education. The Sherpa, unlike Westerners, do not feel that schooling will have any importance in their future—a future that they must carve out of the new Nepalese democracy. If they are to represent themselves, they need a knowledge of how the Nepalese system works.

9

Expeditions and Trekking

The peak is in sight, the wind has dropped, and you know that you are going to make it. You glance over to your Sherpa guide and his smiling face assures you that you are right. You have done what few have been able to do; you have battled the elements and the mountain and you have won. Exhilaration fills your soul and you are truly a happy being. But at what cost have you done this? Perhaps before we get around to the pros and the cons we should take a closer look at expeditions. (Expeditions go to the summits; treks are on trails to look at the peaks.)

The first stories of Sherpas participating in expedition work begin in 1907. Dr. A. M. Kellas wanted to do some climbing in Sikkim (then an independent nation) and he hired several Sherpas from Darjeeling as his high-altitude porters (Kohli 1962). Expedition work did not actually start in Nepal until 1949 when the borders were finally opened to climbers. Until that time Sherpa porters had been recruited in Darjeeling and then taken to Tibet.

Sherpas are well-suited to this job because they are acclimatized to the high altitudes. Though Sherpas can and do get mountain sickness, it is a good bet that they will not, and, unlike lowlanders, they can also maintain their strength at high altitudes. It is not easy climbing through the moraine, the rocks deposited by glaciers. The green ice, snow, frozen rivers and crevasses are continual traps. Just lying awake at Everest Base Camp listening to the ice breaking is enough to send any stout fellow back from where he came.

Some Sherpa women do accompany expeditions and treks. They are usually porters or cook assistants. However, my friend, Pasang from Bhuwa/Shurkey, a woman of about thirty-two who has had three children, has attempted Everest three times. (She and her husband, Lhakpa Sonam, own a trekking company, as mentioned in chapter 8.) On her third try, Pasang came within 311 feet of the top but had to turn back because of high winds. Although it may seem that it would have been worth it to crawl the last few hundred feet, the winds are so powerful that they can pick you up and send you right into Tibet and an early grave. Pasang does hold a world record for staying overnight at 27,770 feet without food, tent or sleeping bag. She and her climbing partner dug a snow cave and waited until the light could show them the way down, because tripping down in the dark would have been just that—tripping all the way down.*

Most Sherpas start on the trails as porters at about the age of twelve, when they can get a work permit. In this way the young boys learn the trails. Eventually they move up to be sherpas. *Sherpa* is both the name of an ethnic group and a job description. A sherpa is one who guides. Every large group has a head sherpa called a *sardar*, and there is usually one Sherpa for every two foreigners. Each group also has a cook, various kitchen workers and other guides. When Sherpas are in the lowlands, they do not carry loads. This is a job now considered beneath their social status. Once having achieved guide status, they only carry loads on expeditions when the group reaches high altitudes (over 20,000 feet).

While no one makes much money, the sardar is paid the most, the cook is next, guides, cook crew and finally the porter in descending order. The pay on expeditions is about three to five times as much as on treks. Expeditions can last up to three months, whereas a typical trek is two to four weeks long.

Most expedition and trekking agencies operate on nepotism. What counts is who you are and who you know. Therefore, most of the people who are working together are probably related or at least know each other. It is unusual to find a Rai or Thamang or other ethnic group guiding with a group of Sherpas.

There is a strict code of honor among the Sherpa who participate in the treks and expeditions. It is quite positively understood that no Sherpa is to step over his bounds of friendship with the foreigners. This usually is not very difficult since Sherpas are very shy, and not knowing a lot of English makes them even shyer. It is also understood that you answer the Sahib's questions

---

*After this manuscript was completed, I learned that Pasang attempted to reach the summit of Everest a fourth time. On April 22, 1993, Pasang became the first Nepalese woman to reach the top of the world's tallest mountain. Her Sherpa male climbing partner had reached the summit for the fifth time. On the way down, however, they encountered a severe snowstorm with dense fog and lost their way. Their bodies were found eight days later. They were taken to Kathmandu and cremated at Swayambhu Temple.

A typical trekking camp; this one is behind a hill at Namche Bazaar and right beside the Sagamartha National Park Museum. Two-person tents are erected by the Sherpas for the tourists. A larger dining tent will also be put up, and beyond the stone wall will be a small latrine tent. The stone hut is used in the summertime by youths who are sent to watch the yaks in their summer meadows. The cook crew also uses this hut for cooking and sleeping when it is available.

A typical trekking lunch: canned meat, chappati (unleavened bread), cooked cauliflower, fresh cabbage, onion and tomatoes with oil dressing. Canned fruit follows.

but that you do not break bread with him. This is usually abided by unless the Sherpa happen to be in a very small group and then they seem to unwind a little. Certainly relations between the sexes are very fragile. Most Sherpa men will make no effort to carry on a conversation with a Memsab—the rest of the crew will tease them unmercifully, if they are caught fraternizing with the female tourists. Most Sherpas who end up with foreign girls meet them in Kathmandu.

One would think that with all the hiking, expedition work and hard farm labor these men perform, they would be wonderful specimens of muscle. In most cases this is not true. They have the thinnest legs I have ever seen. It is difficult to imagine that those legs could take them anywhere, but they do. My husband's muscular legs are one of the few exceptions that I saw.

Nepal has opened 122 peaks out of 1310 peaks above 18,000 feet for international climbers. A foreigner who wants to participate in a trek or expedition must first obtain a permit. The prices have risen dramatically since the new government took over in 1990. Three hundred and forty-three climbers have made it to the top of Everest since 1953, when Hillary and Tenzing Norgay became the first to reach the summit. On May 8, 1991, almost forty years later, the first all-Sherpa expedition made it to the top.

Sundare Sherpa reached the summit of Everest five times—a world record at that time. King Birendra Bir Bikram Shah Dev (who has been in office since January 31, 1972) was so impressed that he offered Sundare a quarter of a million rupees ($8,620) as a reward. Sundare turned the money down and told the king to give it to the monasteries, which the King did. Sundare, however, had a short climbing career. He was an alcoholic. One day while inebriated, and crossing one of the famous suspension bridges in the Himalayas, he fell to his death. (Ang Rita of Khumjung now holds the world record for reaching the summit—seven times.)

My husband has twice been on expeditions to Everest but he has never gotten out of Base Camp. You must be chosen to go to the higher altitudes. Phurba did succeed in reaching the summit of Dhaulagiri (26,810 feet), the sixth tallest mountain in the Himalayas, without the aid of oxygen tanks. Once he, along with another man, worked as a mail runner for an Everest expedition. Every other week one of them would walk down to Lukla, then fly to Kathmandu with mail, and then bring mail back. It is rather ridiculous that they could not just take the mail to Lukla and send it there at the airport; however, Nepal does not seem to have a functioning postal system. In order for us to communicate with our family in Nepal, we send mail to someone in Kathmandu, and then they give it to someone who is going up the mountain. The second person might then have to find a third person to actually deliver it to the Mama. I have recently started to FAX my letters to Kathmandu to be sent to Mama, since most mailed letters do not arrive in Nepal—they are either lost or stolen. If you place a colorful American stamp on a letter it is as good as gone—people will steal the letter for the stamp. Also, if the letter has any thickness to it, people think that it contains money so they steal it. These circumstances do not necessarily prevail in Nepal itself, but can occur in various countries through which the mail is processed.

In addition to communication difficulties and the complex planning needed for a high climb, expeditions sometimes have to take into consideration not only weather and logistics but also superstition. If a Sherpa, while on expedition, dreams something inauspicious, he will not climb. Usually a Sherpa will consult a lama before the expedition. The lama reads the *Dhadur* and determines whether or not it will be propitious for the person to participate. Sherpas like to start a climb on an advantageous day: Mondays or Wednesdays, or perhaps the day of the week on which they were born.

Pink Toilet Paper and Kerosene

Expeditions have many benefits for Nepal in general and the Sherpa in particular. Economically they have injected great amounts of money into the Nepalese economy. In Kathmandu, for example, climbers must purchase food, lodging, equipment, and government permits. Insurance is purchased by the expeditions in case of accident or death. This is not for the foreigners but for the employees of the trekking companies. On expeditions there is no end of ways that Sherpas can die or get injured. Once, when I was staying in the village, a Korean expedition passed through. One of the porters had fallen off a bridge and broken his leg. He was being taken on a stretcher to Lukla. Afterward, he was flown down to the hospital in Kathmandu. The expedition paid for everything including the wages he would have made until his leg mended. If there is a Sherpa death while climbing, the family will receive about two thousand dollars in compensation.

Then, of course, money comes in the hiring of the guides and porters. Naturally, along the way to the base camp the foreigners spend money in the local tea shops. Another benefit occurs when the expedition is finished and the foreigners leave everything behind. At the end of an expedition it is far too costly to ship everything back. What do most of the foreigners want with the gear anyway? So they liberally give it to the Sherpas. In houses all up and down the Solu Khumbu there are containers from expeditions. It is amazing to see the amount of plastic goods the people have. On expeditions the Sherpas are provided with all the equipment that they will need. Therefore, they rarely keep anything other than a pair of boots, sleeping bag and goggles. Even these they will get again on the next expedition. They take most of the expensive gear to Kathmandu and sell it to the trekking shops. There seems to be a trekking shop on every corner, selling all kinds of expensive, top-grade Western equipment for bargain prices (it may need to be cleaned, however). In these ways, the Sherpas gain even more income from the expedition.

Sherpas do this work not because they like it, but because they want to feed their families. The stored food from the farms often runs out long before the fields produce more food. So, for several months, the people must buy food from the lowlanders, who, because of a tropical climate, can grow food year round. The Sherpas must get the money for the food from somewhere, and the dangers of the expeditions are far outweighed by the necessity for the money. The Sherpas will go trekking but only as a secondary job.

Of course, many circumstances present argument against the expeditions. First is the loss of life. Not that many Sherpas have died in expeditions, especially when you compare the figure to the number of driving fatalities in the United States for just one day. Of the 115 climbers who have died on Everest only 43 have been Sherpas (Carrier 1992). On the other hand, even a few deaths out of the small Sherpa population is harmful to the society. What will the death of the primary member of the family do to that family, especially if all the children are small?

In the fall of 1992 we learned that Mapa, a man from Bhuwa/Shurkey and personal friend of mine as well as Phurba's, had died in an expedition to Kanchenjunga. The trekking company for which he had worked is the one owned by his sister Pasang and her husband, Lhakpa Sonam. Mapa was twenty-seven years old and left a pregnant wife and three small children. His wife received the two thousand dollars in insurance. I am sure she benefited from receiving the money, but only in the short-term for with four small children, she will find it difficult to find another husband. I remember the times that Mapa's toddlers climbed into my lap as we drank tea with him and his wife. I wonder what their lives are like now and how they will be ten years from now?

I have no medical evidence to back up my assumption, but I believe many Sherpas go back home after the fifth or sixth or twelfth expedition in weakened health. Hearts beat much faster the higher you go. Surely repeated months of this would strain the health of a person. My father-in-law, whom I never met, came home from an expedition and died three days later. Did he have altitude sickness? Perhaps. Who knows? He was coughing a lot, but all Sherpas cough, especially in high altitudes. My guess is that he had a heart attack. He was forty-six.

Leaving families alone for long periods of time in the spring and fall places an additional burden on those left behind. All work must still be done. If a man leaves his young wife with small children and no other men in the household, she has a real problem. Some men reside in Kathmandu all spring and fall just trying to find work. The expense of this waiting period is a further burden. Mostly the men try to stay with relatives so their board is free, but they must pay for food.

Contact with Western culture has certainly changed many things in Sherpa society. There are both positive and negative effects. Practically all Sherpa men now wear Western clothing. As mentioned earlier, women have managed to maintain the traditional clothing styles, even those women who live in Kathmandu. However, many of the traditions themselves are being changed because of contact with the West. Values, too, are changing. Some Sherpa men have left their families, married foreign women, and moved to the West. My marriage to Phurba still raises questions in my mind. Certainly my Sherpa husband enjoys living in the United States, but he deeply misses his family and friends. However, we can monetarily help his family so much better by living here and not there. It is a two-sided coin. If we lived there, could I adapt to their way of life? More likely I would try to change the life of the village. If I tried to "improve" things and make life more comfortable for myself, what would that do to their culture?

The introduction of Western products can benefit some people, but I mostly view this situation as negative, since most items will need batteries or some kind of maintenance, which will cost additional money. I hate to see the Sherpa caught in a money trap.

Trash! One climbing expedition can leave as much as eleven hundred pounds of trash. Everest Base Camp looks like a trash dump with as much as fifty tons of accumulated garbage. Oxygen cylinders left behind by Hillary in 1953 are still evident at the base camp. ("Clean Himalaya" 1991). The only thing that saves the mountain beauty is the new layers of snow. Several ideas have emerged to solve this problem. The combustible materials could be burned, but the Sherpas believe that burning trash causes bad spirits. Expeditions have been encouraged to carry out their trash, but, in the absence of a compelling reason, they will not. The Nepal Mountaineering Association has proposed that expeditions pay large deposits which they will only get back when they prove that they have brought their garbage back with them. The odious sight of Kathmandu pink toilet paper along every trail has inspired many to campaign for passage of garbage legislation.

A Munich-based mountaineering and trekking agency run by Gunter Strum has developed a Dreck Sack, trash bag. This DAV Summit Club is trying to inspire Europeans to clean up after themselves ("The Dreck Sack" 1991).

The Mountain Protection Commission of the International Union of Alpinist Associations met in Kathmandu on May 8, 1992. Those in attendance agreed to try to reduce litter on mountains and trails and to clean up areas that are particularly troublesome ("Carrying Capacity" 1992). How they plan to do this was not stated. Fines can be levied, but there is no manpower to oversee and monitor the groups before they leave the country.

Mohan S. Kohli, an Indian mountaineer and a commission member, is pessimistic about the foreign agencies' campaigns to clean up Everest. He wants a more permanent effort rather than the one-shot approach. The agencies get great publicity in the West but they really carry out a very small amount of the total accumulated garbage. What is needed is a permanent system of trash removal.

As of May 1992, the Himalaya Environmental Trust has published a "code of conduct" for trekkers and mountaineers. These are suggestions concerning how to act on expeditions and treks. Of course, many people do not take these suggestions well. There are 120 trekking agencies in Nepal, and getting all of them to comply to the simplest commonsense ideas, such as garbage removal and burning of kerosene, will be an uphill battle.

Lastly, there is the whole issue of deforestation. Expeditions and trekking agencies must stop using native wood. In the low altitudes the Sherpa have deforested for their own purposes. In the middle altitudes many areas are still well forested, but in the high elevations every tree that is cut is a disaster. It takes far too long to grow a tree that burns so quickly. Kerosene and stoves must be carried in and are usually the order of the day now.

A Note on Trekking

I love to trek. I would be on the trails constantly if I lived in the Himalayas, and I frequently went before I found my Sherpa husband. Phurba does not care if he ever sees a trail again. To me it was fun, a hobby, a vacation. To him it was just back-breaking, boring work.

The concerns surrounding the influx of foreign trekkers are not much different than those surrounding the expeditions; they are just on a smaller scale. If the trash can be controlled, the economic return will far outweigh the negative contributions. Let us face it, there is no way in this world that we can stop the encroachment of Western civilization. It is far better to try to mold it to help the people affected the most.

The one aspect of trekking that needs altering is the wages paid to the Sherpa workers. Trekking will become an even more expensive sport, but perhaps that is good, as it will decrease the number of people arriving daily. It would be nearly impossible to expect people to stay away voluntarily from the mountains, so that the local inhabitants will not be disturbed. Government restrictions do not always work either; besides much good can be gotten from the trekkers. Many people trek by themselves, especially Europeans and Australians. Perhaps this is one area where the government needs to make some restrictions. The Nepalese and the Sherpas benefit very little from someone who hoists his own pack, cooks his own food, and finds his own way down the trails.

I will never forget my first trek; it was an experience of a lifetime. The corn stood twelve feet tall as I struggled up through the tiny village. The potatoes had already been dug but the buckwheat sprouted beneath the drying corn shocks. Here and there a pole as high as the corn held the tendrils of still blossoming beans. I could see a dahlia pointing its pink blossoms to the sky. The side of the trail was sprinkled with flowering weeds. Surely they all had names—but I just did not know them yet. Many I recognized from back home. I was surprised to be half a world away and yet discover that so much seemed similar.

I looked up from the rocks of the trail to see a Sherpa woman beside the stream I was following. As I passed by, her face held a curious look. I wondered what she thought of me in shorts and T-shirt, carrying a backpack, sweat dripping off my nose as I struggled up the hill. With great ease she would hoist her bamboo-plaited basket filled with forage for the cattle. I probably could not lift it with both hands, but she placed the tump line around her forehead and climbed with amazing grace the same trail upon which I struggled. I felt like an invader from an outside world, a place she would find hard to comprehend. She will probably never travel to my world but it must often seem that the world comes to her as she stands quietly and watches us outsiders struggle by her path. Trekkers and mountaineers from almost every advanced nation take to the trails to challenge themselves against the spectacular Himalayas.

The trails are the primary avenues by which Nepal has become increasingly westernized. Leaving aside issues of modernization, the Nepalese and the Sherpas must somehow learn to balance the economic gains with the cultural and ecological pressures that the expeditions and trekking bring.

10

What Is in the Future?

The Road from Jiri to Namche Bazaar

One misty, chilly August morning, while heading south on Route 30 out of the New York Adirondacks, my husband casually mentioned that a road was going to be built from Jiri to Nauche/Namche Bazaar. My immediate response was, "Oh no, how terrible."

Phurba said that "they" had been to the village several times about four years ago to survey for the road. The Chinese are supposed to fund its building. Due to a history of poor government and now a new government struggling to survive, major projects have needed outside assistance. There are few roads outside the Kathmandu Valley. One leading west to Pokhara was completed in the 1965 with Chinese aid. The major eastward road was just recently extended to Jiri with Swiss aid. Now, according to Phurba, there were plans to extend this road further. The miles involved are very difficult to estimate since the road must switch back and forth up the mountains. However, it would climb from Jiri at 6,250 feet to Nauche/Namche Bazaar at 11,305 feet, a 5,056 foot difference, between which there would many ups and downs since in this section of Nepal the Himalayas run north-south and the road would be running east-west. It would also ford four major rivers. Frequently, adequate bridges are not built and vehicles are left to make their way across as best they can.

I am not primarily concerned with the logistics of building the

95

Namche Bazaar is built in a dishbowl of earth. The houses are on the hills and the fields occupy the only flat land—the center of the village. Many of these homes have become stores, tea shops and hotels. The wall in the background was erected by the landowner so that the Sagamartha National Park would not claim the land.

road but with the impact on the culture, economy and ecology of the area. I suppose it depends on one's perspective as to whether the impact of such a project is seen as beneficial or detrimental. For those living in the area it would mean that there would be less travel time between villages. Locals could reach Kathmandu and home again more conveniently. If they purchased goods, these could be carried on buses or trucks instead of on people's backs. More products would come north on the road—but I wonder about the price of those products. Today a man must be paid to carry the products up the trails. Would the road lower or raise the price? Thinking about the flow of goods south is not very encouraging. Since the climate to the south is tropical, there is little that could be traded from north to south.

The road would also mean that some families would be displaced. Farms are very small in these hills and it is possible that a farmer's entire field could be taken. Farmers would be compensated, of course, but how long would that last? Could the money buy another farm? The road, logically, should be put at the edge of such places to allow a farmer to retain as much of his land as possible, but, will that happen? Many families own various fields in different villages, so with the compensation from one farm they could move to another, provided that the new farm is large enough for their family.

The one transitory benefit that the people will discover is employment. As the road is being built, and it could take years, local people will be employed. In Nepal most work is done by hand, even the spreading of asphalt. Once the road is finished, however, the work will end. As anyone who has traveled the road from Kathmandu to Pokhara can attest, once the road is completed there is little repair work ever done. Once the initial funding has been spent, the government does not allocate any more for repairs.

As to the negative side, all I can smell is diesel fumes. I once took a journey up the Srinagar-Leh Highway in Kashmir, India. It is an area much like the Jiri-Nauche/Namche Bazaar area. The region through which it passes is sparsely populated. The road cut a journey of weeks into mere days; however it does not seem possible to escape the diesel fumes. The large Indian-built Tata trucks never seemed to be serviced and constantly belched unctuous fumes. What might this do to the pristine environment of the Solu Khumbu?

Trucks traversing this road would have to haul something valuable to make the journey profitable. Could that possibly mean lumber? Hillary has become world famous for his efforts to stem the deforestation that is occurring in the Solu Khumbu region. He believes that destroying the environment will only compound more deleterious effects (Hillary 1984). My own husband has told me that the people in his area cut down only the lumber they need, and that strict taboos have controlled the forests for hundreds of years. Unfortunately, as in countless other places around the world, greed will probably win out and the old taboos will be forgotten when someone is offered "big money" for the trees.

The major money makers of the area are the tea shops. The trails are filled with trekkers who have come to see the mountains. These people stop in the tea shops to refresh themselves, buy items from the tiny stores, and sometimes stay in the lodges. A journey of eight days for the trekker will soon become two for the truck. (I really doubt that buses will be able to make the higher elevations past Jiri.) This means that many foreigners will no longer go trekking, and the owners of the tea shops will lose the small income they had gained from the visitors. The new road could mean that at the end of the first day's journey a large town would grow. Hoping to "strike it rich," people would move into the town from the smaller villages, so that they could set up their businesses; thus, the villages would be reduced to ghost towns. Lukla is a prime example of this.

Lukla is the only major airstrip in the Khumbu region. Over the years it has been transformed from a small farming community to a center of tea shops. It seems that everyone's house is a tea shop. In 1989 we visited friends in Lukla who were ever so proud to show us their newly completed house, the majority of which was a tea shop and lodge.

In places where rapid growth takes place without planning there is the inevitable squalor. It would be enchanting to come upon a well-planned, clean, quaint village; however, one's journey is more likely to end in a town like countless others across the world: dirty, disorganized, and dangerous.

What would this road mean to the Sherpa guides and porters? Less work probably. The road would eliminate six days' pay at least. The Sherpas might get paid to ride along and set up camp and cook, but certainly the porters would not be needed. Could the lowlanders afford to walk or ride to Nauche/Namche Bazaar to begin treks there? That might mean more money for the local economy, as Sherpas are forced once again to shoulder the loads. Overall, however, it could mean shorter treks and loss of pay.

What of the animals of the area? I found that most animals are already staying away from the trails because of the constant flow of people. I do not believe that the roads would do much more harm unless the noise and fumes would force them even further away. It might even help the villagers living along the road to prevent problems with bears and other animals eating their crops and killing their animals.

What about the tourists? Those who walk to Nauche/Namche Bazaar from Jiri could then ride. It would be cheaper than flying into Lukla. Also, the flights into Lukla are very vulnerable to weather conditions. I have seen as many as two hundred trekkers waiting in Lukla for flights back to Kathmandu. It is sometimes a week or more before a flight occurs, upsetting everyone's schedule. The road would mean a more dependable means of transportation, although there are obvious problems there. Would there be automotive garages, tire shops and gas stations along the way? What of landslides, floods, potholes and the like? Who would do the necessary repair jobs? Few Sherpas are now trained in motor repair or road repair.

It is a tremendous strain on a tourist's body to fly into Lukla at 9,300 feet or drive into Nauche/Namche Bazaar at 11,305 feet. Walking in from Jiri's 6,250 feet after having become adjusted to Kathmandu's 4,400 feet ensures that altitude sickness can probably be avoided. Arriving suddenly at higher elevations adds to the risk of mountain sickness. If the tourist and trekking companies want to minimize the probability of mountain sickness, then the trekker

Porters are seen hiking up a typical trail in the Khumbu. Villagers sometimes add stones to the trail to complement its natural stone steps. All goods, whether for the villagers or for the tourists, are brought up the trails in this fashion. One porter carries from 60 to 150 pounds.

should have at least one rest day somewhere halfway between Jiri and Nauche/Namche Bazaar and another upon arrival. Mountain sickness is not something to take lightly, as I learned with my own severe cases of both pulmonary edema and cerebral edema almost to the point of death. Still, it is very hard to convince trekkers that these days are essential, especially if there is nothing much to do at these locations. People with limited vacation time want to be in and out as quickly as possible. Trekking companies can arrange for the rest days and force the trekkers to abide by them, but there are many people who trek on the trails by themselves. I foresee even more deaths with the construction of this road.

Then there are the expeditions. Planners of such would welcome the elimination of six days' travel time, but there is still the danger of mountain sickness. It will probably increase if the road is built, since expeditions will be going to even higher elevations to set up their base camps (at around 20,000 feet). Expeditions must bring a tremendous amount of equipment and food. Sometimes

hundreds of porters are needed. The road could work for and against
an expedition. The expeditions will not need to find porters for the
eight days' travel from Jiri to Nauche/Namche Bazaar, but once in
Nauche/Namche Bazaar they would be needed. Would there be
enough Sherpas available? A smaller group of porters would have
to make several trips each—meaning that the days saved by
travelling the new road would be lost and the supplies would have
to be well packed so that the necessary equipment would arrive
before the people. The expeditions might have to pay the porters
to come along so that they could carry the supplies when the road
ended; thus, the expeditions would have the additional cost of the
porters' transportation.

Will the road actually be built? When? How long will it take?
What will be its impact on the people and wildlife of the region?
If only all could be seen before ruination takes place. Unfortunately,
bureaucracy rarely takes those long, deep looks. Another country
gave the government the money to build the road, and it will be
used no matter what the cost.

Micro-Hydro Power

With all the water that rapidly flows down the Himalayas, it
makes sense that water power should be used by everyone. The
largest problem, as always, is money. Few local people have the
money to afford turbines, transformers and wiring. The government
is not relied upon because earlier bureaucrats had mismanaged
energy planning (Gyawali 1991). The new government, while
struggling to define itself, will undoubtedly be no better. Most of
the governmental plans involve the lowlands, which seems logical
since most of the people live there. Right now Kathmandu is
growing so rapidly that there is no way that water power can fill
the energy needs of the entire city. It is quaint to find a candle in
your hotel room, and you may be able to put up with a loss of power
for an evening, but imagine what it would be like to live under such
circumstances all the time. More importantly, industry cannot abide
infrequent power. No wonder no one builds factories in Nepal.

Water power would be wonderful for the villages. It could mean
a decrease in the amount of fuel wood consumption and provide
power for small village industries, as well as make life a lot easier
for the average villager. Try to imagine your world without
electricity. Has the power ever gone out for a substantial period of
time in your house? What have you been able to do? What have
you not been able to accomplish?

There are micro-hydro projects sponsored by the Agricultural

Development Bank (ADB/N) (Pfaff-Cazarnecka 1991) that grants loans to villagers who want to put in turbines. The turbines are primarily used to grind grain and make oil—presumably the villagers who receive the loans charge a fee to any person who wants to take advantage of the ready electricity. Theoretically, electrification of houses can be added. However, if the houses are more than a kilometer away from the turbine, a transformer must also be purchased. Because of voltage fluctuation in this system, light bulbs rapidly burn out and cause additional money problems for the villagers. The biggest problems occur when the equipment breaks down and no one knows how to repair it or when spare parts cannot be found.

Most of the villagers are not aware of all the possible government agencies that could provide them with grants and loans for instituting the micro-hydro projects. On the other hand, many of these grants and loans are dependent on politics, so even if the villagers do apply they may never receive anything. Foreign aid can be used for such projects, but, because the money is "free," the government and people do not use it as wisely as if it were their own. Graft is rife in Nepal.

There is another argument here, also—the decay that accompanies the unwise application of electricity. In my classroom I have often seen the negative effects of television. Because television says it, students reason, then it must be true; because television shows it, then it must be acceptable. If television is introduced on a mass scale, much of the Sherpa way of life may be altered. The visiting of neighbors in the evenings will stop, just as it did in the United States. Intervillage visiting will stop, or at least be severely truncated. All the many daily activities—such as storytelling and games for the children—will be subjugated to television. The children will learn other values and discard their own. Adults will begin to demand the new products they see. They will begin to substitute the values of the television for their own. If the programs are let to go unchecked, as in the United States, then entire cultures may disappear.

Today many villages already have electricity. In the Solu, Salleri, the district headquarters, has electricity. Phaplu and Chyalsa in the Solu also have it. In the Khumbu, Nauche/Namche Bazaar and recently Lukla have electricity. Thangboche Monastery was electrified but burnt to the ground in January 1989 due to poor wiring.

Foreign Assistance

Many nations are making efforts to help the people in third world countries. I think they are wonderful, just not large enough.

In 1982 I met a Peace Corps worker in Nauche/Namche Bazaar who was trying to give an adequate water supply to the town. The water source was located downhill from the village. This meant that the children and women were carrying the water uphill to meet their daily needs, an incredible task. The Peace Corps worker had installed rubber hoses with a generator to pump the water up to the village. The only problem was that the generator was always failing. When I met the Peace Corps worker, he was trying to teach several Sherpas how to repair the generator so that when he left they would be able to repair it themselves. He had yet to address the problem of obtaining spare parts.

Lots of villages are now using rubber hoses to pipe their water in the summer. If the water is flowing downhill, people can easily have running water in their houses. However, in winter they will have to go back to carrying the water themselves, since low temperatures will cause any water in the pipes to freeze and burst the pipes. Several houses in Bhuwa/Shurkey have rubber piping; Mama is not located in an area where the water can be gravity-fed, so the boys still have to carry it to the house on their backs. Transporting water seems to be a job for the young. The first time I saw seven-year-old Nha Temba carrying a five-gallon plastic jug of water up the hill from the stream, I asked my husband why he or the older brothers did not help. His reply was, "I did it at his age."

The building of simple methane plants is an easy task. The problem is always to convince the people that they should do this. Even if they see the benefit of something new, they may go back to the "old ways" when the foreign workers leave. Methane can be produced from manure. After being processed in a methane plant, the manure can still be used as fertilizer. Installing a methane power plant in our village would mean that the villagers will have to change the way they handle manure. As I have stated, we let ours build up in the stable over the year. Methane production would involve gathering the manure daily.

Sanitation is also a problem. Sherpas do not know about germs. It is difficult to get people to wash their hands or build a privy, if they do not understand why they should. In my mother-in-law's house the family rarely washes the dishes with anything but cold water; soap is not usually used. People prepare meals after they have done stable chores. The floor always seems to be filthy. Living on a farm and having to go through the barn to get to the second floor means that all kinds of material is tracked upstairs. The floor is swept two or three times a day, but it is never scrubbed. Some houses have privies. Mama had one but the little building, made from bamboo, has disappeared. Since it was right beside the house, I could not help but feel conspicuous. The river banks along frequently used trails are a mess from human excrement; Nepalese like to wash themselves after eliminating and they do not use toilet paper. Foreigners use toilet paper which is probably worse. There you are, hiking away in midmorning along a trail. Suddenly you have to go to the bathroom. You are in the middle of nowhere, no villages in sight. Camp, with its latrine tent, is many hours down the road. What do you do? Naturally you head into the forest, pick a bush and deposit your paper. What you should do is go far, far off the trail, and when you are finished, bury your offensive material and either burn (be careful not to start a forest fire), bury, or carry your messy paper with you.

In the Helambu region east of the Solu Khumbu, I came upon an area that had been devastated by a great forest fire. Since this area was sparsely populated, it was probably due to lightning. For more than a day I walked beside the once-great forest, which had been entirely charred. At camp that evening we could hear axes biting into the trees and numerous men singing as they gathered the wood. The Sherpa had made something positive out of the misfortune. The forest would eventually regrow, even if it would take a long time.

Currently there is very little garbage in the villages. Everything is either fed to the animals or made into compost. As the Sherpa villages absorb more foreign goods, such as paper and plastics, then there will be a garbage problem. Most of the garbage seen in Nepal today is the result of Westerners. However, I have found that the villagers also have little regard for proper disposal of garbage. Combustible garbage is not burned in Sherpa houses, because they feel it causes bad spirits. I have watched members of my family throw pieces of paper or tin cans out the window. Later I retrieved the garbage but had nowhere to dispose of it. At the time I tried to explain to my husband the necessity of proper disposal, but he looked at me as if I were crazy. Kathmandu is a mess. Some refuse is thrown into the streets as fodder for the sacred cows, although much of it is not eaten. Other garbage is just thrown where convenient. After living in the United States, my husband has begun to appreciate what I mean by a clean environment (however, I cannot bring all of the Nepalese and Sherpa to the United States).

Foreign organizations can really help the villagers by introducing more efficient farming methods. Even though the Sherpas have been farming for hundreds of years, they are using the same methods—nothing seems to have changed. One caution should be noted when working with the Sherpas: if they are to change to new methods, they must be clearly shown some immediate benefit or they will not even attempt the change. Improved crops, such as the new strain of potato recently introduced, can be a blessing, as long as the people can get the seed or—as in the case of potatoes—produce their own.

Certainly there would be no medical aid in the mountains, if it were not for foreign assistance. The Kunde Hospital, the only one in the Khumbu, was built by Hillary in 1966. Doctors, nurses and aides are being trained, but an impossible hurdle for them is an adequate supply of medicine. Even in Kathmandu medicines are impossible to get and very expensive when available. However, even with the proper use of medications, some problems still cannot be solved—worms, for example. The medicines that cure one of worms are fairly cheap and the patient only has to take four pills to be rid of six different kinds of worms; however, as soon as the individual drinks the water he or she is infected again. An additional problem occurs in transporting people to the hospital. As previously stated, getting an ailing individual to the hospital is a task that is often not accomplished before death.

As one considers all the things that could and should be done in Nepal, it boggles the mind. It sometimes sounds easier and better just to say that these people should stay the way they are. Of course, this is naive and impossible. The AIDS virus had reached Nepal by 1989. By the summer of 1991 there were twenty-four known cases: ten Nepalese women, eight Nepalese men and six foreigners. The women had mostly contracted the disease in Indian brothels. In a country with little or no education about AIDS the disease will spread rapidly. There is no place in this world that can just be left alone. However, how change will come about and who will direct it are very real problems.

11

What About Phurba?

So, how is it that we managed to be together? It is not a really long story, but it is a different one. I had begun going to Nepal in 1982. Being a history major in college and a history teacher for many years, I am fascinated with certain periods of history. One I enjoy is ancient Egyptian history, and by 1977 I had seen all the major finds up and down the Nile. The second is my passion for Tibet and its people; however, traveling to Tibet is very expensive for a teacher. Then I found Nepal, where the Tibetan Sherpas live, but it was impossible to go to in the summer because of the monsoon—or so I thought.

In 1982 I was furloughed from teaching so I took the opportunity to go to Nepal. I figured I would never again have the opportunity to travel so far so I decided, as many do, to see Mount Everest. How could I possibly say that I had been to the Himalayas and not seen Mount Everest? The way was long and hard. Since there were no roads, I had to walk or trek to see the mountains and the people. It was very difficult for me. I had taken a plane into Lukla at 9,300 feet. (While gazing out over the Lukla airstrip I had no idea that my husband-to-be's village was just one hour downhill.) Having lived all my life at sea level, this wreaked havoc on my internal organs. Our Western guide, a nincompoop if there ever was one, had suggested that we wear our heaviest clothing for the flight. We sweltered for hours in the Kathmandu airport, and upon arrival at Lukla we found it to be a sprightly sixty degrees Fahrenheit. It was this kind of misleadership that nearly cost me my life.

Off we went uphill, forever uphill. In three days we were well above 12,000 feet. I began to throw up, would not eat, would sleep constantly in camp, had a headache and could not seem to focus my mind. Any amateur could tell you that I had altitude sickness. (That I was suffering from pulmonary edema and cerebral edema is also evidenced by the fact that I can hardly remember those three days of my life.) Our supposedly well-informed emergency medical technician and guide proclaimed the flu. They loaded me onto a yak and led me ever uphill to the Gokyo Lakes at 16,000 feet. Now the simple cure for altitude sickness is to take the person down in altitude immediately. If done so at that time, I would have been perfectly all right. Eventually we came back down to 12,000 feet. I was planning to go up the Khumbu valley (18,000 feet) with the others, but it was decided that I was too weak and that I should stay in the village and wait for the others to return.

Coincidentally, a man was also sick. The guide thought he was having a heart attack so a helicopter had been ordered for him. (It turned out to be pulled rib cage muscles.) When the helicopter arrived, I begged to be taken aboard and eventually got home to medicine. I had the pulmonary edema eleven days before I saw the doctor. He said that people usually die in the first week. So I had been really, really lucky.

That should have been that. No sane, logical person would ever return. Right? Perhaps it was that I did not finish—I did not prove to myself that I could do it—that sent me back once again to the mountains. I found Ladakh, in northern India. Its far northern location means that the monsoon does not reach Ladakh, making it a perfect place to visit in the summer. Ladakh is Tibetan. So in the summer of 1984 I toured Ladakh and even ventured on a ten-day hike. At Christmastime I went back to Nepal for a short hike in the Annapurna region. In 1987 I left teaching and was able to trek the long and difficult Annapurna Circuit. Finally, in 1988 I chose to hike the Jugal Himal.

I chose the Jugal Himal because it was a little-known hike. I had been on the trails where all the tourists go and I wanted to get away into little-known territory. The first days of the trek were along a ridge where there were no villages at all. How wonderful it was to be in the wild Himalayas, I thought—alone, practically, except for our little group. We were eight trekkers, a guide, three Sherpa, a cook and two helpers, and about twelve to fifteen porters. Not actually alone, but I liked the security of the group as well.

We left Kathmandu traveling in a peculiar, stocky bus. It had one bench seat in the front and two benches along the sides with an open space in the rear. My roommate and I were lucky enough to get the front seat for the beginning of the journey. The rest of the trekkers sat on the benches; in the back were our duffle bags, all the other equipment, and the crew scattered wherever they could fit. We started our journey and found the road to be the typical

Nepalese road: in poor repair. We jostled, bumped and bounced our way along. For some reason I turned around in my seat and looked toward the back of the bus. At the same precise moment one of the Sherpas, who had been sleeping with his head down on one of the duffle bags, lifted his head and looked up toward the front of the bus. I can remember thinking, "How can that man sleep? Look at those eyes!"

When we arrived at the end of the road, our first camp site, I could not help but notice this same Sherpa when he shed his pants and, in shorts, began to put up the tents. Muscular legs, so uncommon to Sherpa men, caught my eye. His legs were not very long but they had huge bulges of muscles and were covered with black hair, unlike most Orientals.

The next day we began the trek. I happened to be one of the people in the front and this Sherpa was the one leading that day. Each day the Sherpas rotated lead, sweep (the last person in the group), and with the porters. We came upon a village and in very broken English this Sherpa told me that he had gotten most of the porters from there. As always there was a festival going on in Kathmandu and, therefore, a shortage of porters, so they had to be gathered from local villages. This was alright, except that on long treks porters would sometimes decide that they had gone far enough from home and quit. Then the sardar would have to find other porters—not always an easy task.

As the days progressed, I found that the three Sherpas were Penoorie (the young sardar), Phurba, (the one I was watching), and Pasang (an older man). I could not help but be drawn to Phurba. When he walked as sweep then I found myself walking very slowly. I would not see him on the days that he walked with the porters, and I found that I was depressed. I felt so foolish, as if I were one of the junior-high-school girls I used to teach who had a huge crush on someone whom did not even know she existed.

When we stopped for a rest, I would try to sit near the Sherpas and try out my limited vocabulary on them. They laughed heartily at me but at that point I did not care. It is difficult to describe what I felt. I did not actually know Phurba, but I found him attractive. He had thick black hair, speckled with gray; a broad, strong nose; a pleasant, ever-smiling mouth that just drew me to him. We giggled constantly with each other, even though we did not know at what we were giggling. I would look into his eyes and see a sparkle that I wanted to know better. I could tell that he was intelligent from how quickly he caught onto my ideas expressed in a few fumbled words and some hand gestures.

Then we came to Nosepati. We were about seven days into the trek and had seven more to go. I decided that if I were going to become more friendly with Phurba, I would have to get him away from his ever-present friend Penoorie. If I could only get Phurba to take a little walk with me in the afternoon after we had reached camp, then maybe I could see if he was as interested in me as I was in him. So when we arrived at Nosepati I had decided to try and do something. Phurba, however, rolled himself up into his sleeping bag and stayed there until supper. I was really upset and could not admit to myself why I was.

The next day we had a hard uphill walk to *Paunch Pokari* (Five Lakes). We stopped frequently, yet Penoorie always seemed to be there. We were going slowly and everyone hiked together that day, so Penoorie, even as sweep, was right along with Phurba in the lead. Penoorie could speak better English than Phurba and so much of the conversation was between Penoorie and me, and Penoorie and Phurba. At one stop I sat right beside Phurba on a rather uneven rock and, as a test, I leaned against his shoulder. He did not seem to mind at all. We walked together and chatted all along the trail. At camp Phurba had to set up the tents—first the individual tents, which housed two trekkers in each, and then the large dining tent. He would also have to dig the latrine hole and set up that tiny tent.

Upon their arrival in camp, most of the trekkers crashed in their tents; some slept, others read, others adjusted clothing. I typically stayed outside and let my tent mate have the time alone in the tent. I was not one for sleeping and I could not face reading a book when I had the Himalayas to look at. So I was standing around, surreptitiously watching Phurba put up the tents. Just as he was finishing the dining tent, two other members of the group came up to me and asked if I wanted to accompany them up the hill to a Buddhist monument that looked out over the lakes. As I looked up to the monument, Phurba was in my sight line. Sure, I would go. As we passed beside Phurba I tapped him and said, "Aaune, aaune" (Come, come). He gazed at me a little bewildered but when I tugged on his arm, he followed me. He was not done with his work, as the latrine tent was not yet up, but he followed me anyway.

We arrived at the top of the short, steep hill in minutes. There we held the customary picture-taking ceremony. Then my fellow travelers moved down the valley to a Hindu shrine. I said that I would stay on the hill for a little longer and Phurba stayed with me. In thirty-five-degrees-Fahrenheit weather with a fairly stiff wind, I sat down. This must surely be love, to endure such conditions. Phurba began to pick tiny leaves. We were above the tree line here and only short, scrubby plant life existed.

"What are they?" I asked. "Yo key ho?"—in Nepalese.

"Rhododendron," was the simple answer.

"Why do you want them?" "Kina?"

"Kathmandu bechnu." "Sell in Kathmandu."

"Religion?" I asked in English.

"Religion." He replied in English and handed me some of the leaves (I still have them).

The conversation was difficult and getting nowhere. Meanwhile, I was beginning to freeze sitting on the cold ground.

"Do Sherpas kiss?" Even to this day I have no idea why I asked that.

"Kess?" I could tell that he had no idea what I was talking about. I knew that Sherpas were not supposed to kiss, but often information such as that is wrong or out of date.

I motioned for Phurba to come nearer to me; he was several feet away. So he came over and sat next to me. I kissed him. I waited for him to pull away or laugh or express horror, but none of that happened. He kissed me again. So we spent a delightful half-hour. He really had not known how to kiss. I was an enthusiastic instructor and he was an excellent pupil. My heart leapt and I could not think.

Later when we sneaked back to camp from opposite directions, I began to think horrible thoughts. I was deeply in love (or was it lust?), but what did he feel? Was it just an unexpected tryst with a tourist? A thrilling half-hour to tell the boys about? I was scared that everyone would start giggling as soon as they saw me. I waited fearfully for supper. Nothing happened. Afterward the Sherpas built a fire for us (not an ecologically acceptable thing to do), and as we sat and sang songs in English and Sherpa, I stole glances at Phurba and though he smiled at me no one else seemed aware that anything was amiss.

I crawled into my sleeping bag that night a very confused individual. There was the problem of age difference. I knew that I was at least ten to fifteen years older than Phurba. I just could not see how anything could possibly work between us. He knew hardly any English and was so unaware of what my world was like.

We spent the next several days trying to talk, sneaking a kiss here and there and holding hands when no one was looking. That amazed me since Sherpas do not hold hands, or so I had been led to believe. I was beginning to hope that he felt a small portion toward me of what I felt for him. At this point I was absolutely sure that my feelings were love. I had never felt this way in my entire life. I felt that I had finally found the person who would make me happy and whom I could make happy. I just worried constantly about what he felt for me. When you can speak to someone in the same language, you rarely know exactly how that person feels about you; imagine what it is like when you do not speak the same language.

At one point I gave Phurba my Gore-Tex jacket to wear, as he did not have any jacket at all and it was quite cold. We were at 14,000 feet and the mornings and evenings were below freezing. It was difficult for people not to notice the jacket, since it was bright turquoise. One of the men in my group commented about the jacket and said that I probably would never get it back.

We spent another delightful day holding hands and working our way up a gradual hill through the mustard fields on the way to Shermatang. Phurba and I arrived at the village gate first, which was still quite some distance from town. It was one of the most beautiful gates I had ever seen, decorated with spectacular, delicate Buddhist paintings. We paused and waited for the rest of our group to catch up with us. It seemed like a magical place.

Upon our arrival at Shermatang, we were told that the village school, a private one, would gladly let us visit. The bliss of the afternoon continued as we in the trekking group watched apple-cheeked youths reciting, singing and dancing. It just could not have been better if it had been planned by the tour company.

We returned to camp, which was sitting above the village on the grounds of a monastery. I sat down on the surrounding wall, which gave an exceptional view of the cascading terraces. It was a bustling Sherpa village. I watched as people moved here and there. I could see signs hanging from houses advertising tea shops and lodges. One structure had HOTEL painted on its tin roof in huge letters. Phurba came and sat down next to me—a very unusual thing for him to do in camp. We looked out over the village and mumbled at each other. I found myself giggling uncontrollably.

"Are you married?" I asked him.

"No. You are." It was not a question.

Yes, I had to admit that I was, but my marriage had failed, although it had not yet legally ended. It was obvious Phurba already knew. Early in the trek we had spent one lunch time sharing pictures of those we had left behind. Pasang, the older Sherpa guide, had watched us and obviously informed Phurba.

"Who will you marry? Will your father decide?" I asked.

"Father dead."

"So it is yours to decide?" Much of this conversation was accompanied with various hand signals to help him understand.

"Yes. Foreign girl." He smiled broadly.

"You want to marry a foreign girl?" I was a little heart broken, at first, because it sounded like any foreign girl would do. Then I hoped that it was just his poor understanding of English. "Do I have a chance?" I seriously doubted that he understood my wording but I pointed to myself at the same time.

Phurba's entire face lit up and he said "Yes." So I interpreted that to mean that he was proposing to me, or perhaps I to him. My heart swelled. Would it be possible that we could be together? Even if I had known then how much we had to overcome, it still would not have stopped me.

Darkness had fallen by the time we ate supper. The dining tent had not been put up because we were to dine on the porch of the very small monastery. Since the lama or lamas were not around that day, we did not get to see the inside until the next morning. Instead, we dined outside on the folding tables that had been put up in one corner of the porch. The one kerosene light threw a thin shadow across the porch paintings. The entire wall of the monastery was covered with the most fantastic, beautiful paintings. It was easy to see that the same person who had painted the village entry gate had been at work here too. However, it was very difficult to see any detail in the soft light, which actually made the experience fairly frightening; the Buddhist figures seemed to be leaping out of the darkness. I was continually looking over my shoulder to make sure that nothing was moving toward me.

Supper was not an easy meal for me that night. I was so beset with the idea of Phurba proposing to me, or I to him, that I could eat very little. The cook had made a special meal for us, taking much time and work, but the thought that went into preparing my dinner was wasted. I glanced over my shoulder again and saw my turquoise jacket at the very edge of the light. Phurba, who never was around at mealtime, stood there during almost the entire meal. He was waiting to escort us down into town after the meal to a house where we would sample chang and Sherpa hospitality. I choose to think that he was afraid that I somehow would not go if he were not there.

When we arrived at the house, the trekkers sat on wooden benches along the wall; the Sherpas sat on the floor in front of us. I noticed that Phurba chased Penoorie away so that he could sit directly in front of me. Phurba was drinking arak out of a teacup, and when he offered me a drink out of his cup I knew that things were going my way. Sherpas do not let others drink out of their cups. When using a water bottle, they pour the water into their mouths without touching their lips to the bottle. So for me to drink from his cup in front of all those people assembled in the house was a very large deal.

We staggered back to camp together that night. In front of everyone he dragged me off into the darkness to a cow shed where we made love. Afterward he whispered the words I wanted to hear, "I love you," but I could not help but doubt that he knew what they meant. He merely copied what I had been saying.

The next day was a nightmare. Phurba was assigned to the

porters for the second day in a row, and I could hear him shouting at Penoorie in the morning. I mooned along the trail like a love-stricken teenager until the guide, a Scotsman, caught up to talk to me. He lectured me on fraternizing with the natives. When I stated that this was not something casual on my part, that I was very serious, he tried to convince me just how impossible my situation was. He assured me that I could never live in Nepal, that Phurba's family would probably try to kill me, that Phurba was already married (!) and that taking Phurba to the United States was legally impossible. He nearly scared me half to death but my love was stronger than fear. Penoorie also walked with me and tried to talk me out of my love. With him I interpreted it as jealousy.

Before I could see Phurba to confront him about this marriage another blow fell. I did not exactly know how to deal with the marriage issue, since I was also technically still married. I was most upset because I had told Phurba I was married but he had not told me that he was. I was afraid that he would not be able to get a divorce; I did not know if there was such a thing in Nepal. Then I thought that he actually did not want to leave his wife and that I had been wrong all along about his feelings for me. The rest of the day was agony as my feelings tore me apart.

When we arrived in camp we had tea and some of the women discussed my problems with me. They were all for me and trying to make things work. The men all seemed to be against me. As the time passed we all realized that Phurba was nowhere to be found and that the tents were not up. Finally, Pasang, the older Sherpa, and some of the cooking crew put up the tents.

Later I pieced together what had happened. At a tea shop that afternoon Phurba and Penoorie had again had words. Behind all their arguing was Penoorie's jealousy, but they had had words over the porters. Penoorie did not like to part with money, but traditionally the trekking companies provided money so that the porters could have chang at the tea shops. Penoorie would not buy the chang for the porters, because he wanted to keep the money for himself. They argued and Phurba bought the chang out of his own pocket. Unfortunately, Phurba drank a little too much. Then, while waiting for the last porter, he fell asleep along the trail. The porter did not see him and passed him. Phurba woke up hours later and got to camp about two hours late. Another very vocal argument between Penoorie and Phurba occurred. However, we English speakers could not make out what was going on since it was in Sherpa. We could tell that Phurba was still drunk and assumed that because Penoorie kept shouting "duty" in English that the argument was over Phurba being drunk and not getting to camp on time.

Phurba returned my jacket to me. He shouldered his pack and as he started over the wall that surrounded camp the guide said that he had quit the trek. "Hurry Donna, follow him," my fellow female trekkers urged. So, with nothing in hand but the extra jacket, I ran off down the trail after Phurba.

We spent a madcap afternoon and evening. We went to a village house and drank chang as I tried to figure out what was going on. Phurba's English was hopeless when he was drunk. We went scurrying to another house and then back again to the original house after about an hour. We had escaped to the second house because our group had come to the first house for tea. The crew arrived and there were long, rather heated discussions. Two of the porters were Sherpas and they had arrived, also. Penoorie was the only Sherpa who was not there. Finally after listening to some of the men, I pieced together what had happened. I had thought that I was in some way the cause. I was actually, but it was all under the scenes. Penoorie was really jealous of Phurba, not because Penoorie liked me but because Phurba was going to have a chance to make a better life. The crew did not realize this. They discussed the events over and over again trying to understand what had actually happened. Everyone was on Phurba's side and against Penoorie, which was not good since Penoorie was the sardar.

The crew left to make supper for the trekkers. We ate with the family. It was really a marvelous interlude, despite the circumstances. I watched the lady of the house cook the supper over a tiny fire on the floor. A toddler in the family threw himself into my lap and demanded that I play with him. It was a welcome respite.

Then the crew arrived again and more drinking and arguing took place. I spent that night with Phurba on a bench-bed on the family's enclosed front porch.

The next morning I returned to the group in time for breakfast. Phurba began to follow us down the trail and the Scottish guide had a confrontation with us. Phurba had quit the crew so he could not walk along with us; he needed to leave.

We tried to straighten out our affairs using Penoorie as an interpreter. How could I trust anything that Penoorie said, after what had happened. Fortunately, it seemed that minor (!) arguments like the day before were quickly mended in Sherpa society. Penoorie assured me that Phurba would come to the hotel when we got back from trekking and that he would come to the United States with me. What about the wife? After concentrated questioning I found that he was married but not happy with the marriage, or so he said. That gave me some small hope.

I spent three dreadful days finishing that trek and wondering if Phurba would really appear in Kathmandu. He was to come to the hotel at three o'clock. At three o'clock Penoorie was there but no Phurba. So we got a taxi and made all the rounds of where Phurba could possibly be. I saw parts of Kathmandu that I did not know existed. In desperation we arrived back at the hotel at half past four just as Phurba rode up on a bicycle. How could he have been on time? He did not have a watch.

Later I was to find out that it was sheer luck that Phurba had appeared on my trek. He had been scheduled to go on an expedition that would give him far more money; however, at the last moment the expedition was cancelled and Phurba was without a job. The only trek his agency could give him started in two days. He went to another agency, run by his uncle, who told Phurba that he could go on a trek the next day. He discussed the alternatives with his friends and they all agreed that he should wait and go with his present agency. For some strange reason Phurba went against all his friends' advice and left the next day on the trek that was mine. How close we came to missing one another. We have also found out that every time I was in Nepal, Phurba was somewhere close to the same area in which I was trekking.

We spent the next year trying to obtain a "normal" life. I went back to the United States and divorce proceedings. Phurba was to obtain a passport and also divorce his wife. Then he would come to the United States. I received only one letter from Nepal in the next three months—since Phurba could not write English he had to get someone to write the letter for him. I was at my wits end so I decided to go to Nepal myself. When I arrived Phurba had succeeded in getting his passport, but nothing had been done about the divorce. During that time I stayed in Kathmandu in an apartment with Phurba and Penoorie. Even though they had fought horribly on the trek, they seemed to have become best of friends. Near the time of Losar we went to the village so that I could meet the family and celebrate the new year with them.

Back in Kathmandu nothing seemed to be progressing, so I consulted a lawyer about the marriage. After many meetings and one horrible confrontation with the wife, the lawyer discovered that Phurba was not really legally married. At the age of eleven a marriage was arranged for Phurba by his father and uncle with an older girl from several villages away. Father thought that the family had money, but it turned out that they did not. Phurba did not want the marriage and he ran away. The uncle found Phurba and they took him to the girl's house, stripped him of his clothes and would not give them back until he slept with the girl. Then Phurba immediately returned home. Phurba was under age at this time, none of the legal or Buddhist ceremonies had been performed, and none of the traditions were observed such as the chang giving and so on. Father had merely declared that Phurba was married and because he was so young, Phurba accepted it as fact. The girl never even came to live in Phurba's house, as is the custom in a traditional marriage. Shortly afterward she moved to Kathmandu, because her relatives could not tolerate her (they had been trying to foist her off on someone else but it had not worked). Phurba never took up residence with her, though he would stay at her apartment in Kathmandu from time to time when he did not have any money and when there was nowhere else to stay. He rarely gave the girl any money; most of what he earned went to his parents. That convinced me and the lawyer that there was no marriage. We felt some pressure from her family to pay them off, but we resisted their attempts at blackmail.

So we got Phurba a visa for the United States and off we went. It was actually a very good thing I was there; Phurba would never have been able to change planes in Frankfort or even figure out to which gate he was to go. I am sure none of the employees working at the information desks would have been able to speak Nepalese.

When we first arrived in the United States, I was afraid that Phurba would not be able to adjust to such a different way of life. Initially, it was very hard because he could not speak English well and he could not work because he had a tourist visa. For a man who is used to working from first light to beyond dusk, it was hard to just sit around. We returned to Nepal when his six-month tourist visa ran out. We could have gotten another visa in the States, but we wanted to see the family again. Mingma, Phurba's brother, had died while we were in the United States, so we needed to pay for the cremation ceremony. Once again Penoorie stayed with us in Kathmandu. He seemed to be a constant friend, or a rather skillful con artist, as he ended up with many of our possessions.

We spent time in the village and then went through the nightmare of trying to get Phurba an emigration visa. It really was not that hard; there was just so much to do, and in third-world countries things move very slowly. We were married by that time so there was no question that he could get the visa; we just had to go through all the necessary requirements. First, there was a birth certificate, an unheard of thing in Nepal. They do not even celebrate birthdays. The U.S. Embassy said that the certificate had to come from the headman of the village, but that was the spurned woman's brother and we were not on speaking terms with the family. Finally, we got a document from Phurba's uncle who was the assistant to the headman. We had to chase him all over the country, since when we were in the village he was in Kathmandu, and when we got to Kathmandu he was nowhere to be found. Then we had to send for the official paper and seal. Finally, it all came together.

The toughest part was to get the police report stating that Phurba had never been in police trouble. The lawyer helped file the necessary papers, but it took weeks of Phurba going to the police station daily and waiting for something to be done. It was an excruciating experience for Phurba, since most Sherpas fear the police greatly. Sherpas are really very timid with "outsiders." The police are especially frightening to them. We were told that Phurba had to sit in the police station and wait for his name to be called; if he was not there, they would throw the paper away. Finally, Phurba ran into Penoorie's uncle who just happened to be a police inspector. When Phurba told him what he had been going through, the uncle marched Phurba back to the police station and in a matter of minutes he was holding the proper paper. It helps to know someone of importance.

We then had to get the standard chest X-ray and blood tests. These, too, turned out to be difficult to obtain, as we were told the blood-test results would not be ready until the day after our scheduled interview with the visa official. It was not an easy matter to change an appointment with a visa official, and the postponement could cause one to miss the allotted visas for that month (Nepal is only allowed to grant so many visas each month). If the visas ran out, then we would have to wait for the next month; hence, we wanted to make that appointment. We went to the hospital and inquired about the tests for four straight mornings. There were some further difficulties because the doctors of Nepal only have office hours in the afternoon. Finally, we received the results—the day before the appointment.

The conditions of the doctor's office and the hospital were incredible. I could not imagine healing taking place in such filthy conditions. I was afraid that Phurba would contract a disease when he got the blood test, but he reassured me afterward that a disposable needle had been used.

Finally, we met with a United States visa official and everything was complete. Back in the States, some four months later, we obtained Phurba's green card, so he can now stay as long as he likes and work, too. My only fear is what will happen if I die first. Most people assume that Phurba will get his United States citizenship, but I do not think that this is a wise idea. If he is a United States citizen when I die and he wishes to return to Nepal, the Nepalese government will probably refuse him residency. Until recently an ex-Nepalese citizen could only obtain a one-month visa to stay in Nepal—the same as any other foreigner. Now it has been changed to three months. If I die, I want Phurba to be able to go back to his family if he chooses. Retaining his Nepalese citizenship would enable him to do that. With the green card he can also choose to stay in the United States if he wishes.

Despite all our differences Phurba and I have built a solid marriage. After four years we are happier than ever. Each day binds us closer as we are able to understand each other more fully. It has been a long, hard road but certainly worth the effort.

We know of only one other Sherpa from Bhuwa/Shurkey in permanent residence in the United States; however, he is some fifteen years older than my husband so he had actually left the village when Phurba was very small. I know all of this man's brothers, sisters and his parents. His sister, Pasang, owns the trekking agency that I first mentioned in chapter 8 and his brother, Mapa, was just recently killed on expedition. We frequently receive phone calls from Sherpas who have received plane tickets to the United States from wealthy tourists on expeditions. It is amazing how many of the Sherpas have traveled to different places around the world. For example, Phurba's best friend, Kami, has been to Belgium.

My husband tells me that he had his eye on me from the very start of the trek, but, because of his status as a worker, he could not really start anything. He was fearful that I would scream and that he would lose his job. So it was a good thing that I had taken matters into my own hands. It is also my Buddhist husband's opinion that we have been together in another life. It did seem as if we recognized each other on first sight. Why did I keep going back to Nepal even though the place had almost killed me? Phurba says it is because I knew that he was there somewhere and that I had to find him.

Concluding Thoughts

The sun slips toward the Western hills as Mama leads us across the village and up the hill to Pemba and Kami's lodge. As we pass the village *mani* wall, I wave to the lady who lives beside it. We will see her and most of the village later for chang. At Pemba and Kami's lodge we are greeted with a broad smile and lots of chatter. Even though we have eaten, we are prodded until we take fried potatoes. Pemba immediately sets china tea cups full of chang in front of the women and glasses for the men, urging us, to "Shay. Shay." Three times we must sip as she refills. We are expected to feign reluctance to drink. The talk bounces happily around the room, laughter erupting frequently. Gradually, more and more people arrive until a great number of people crowd the room. These impromptu gatherings take place almost every evening in the periods of little work. Tomorrow we will probably be at Pasang Rinzee's across the river.

It is a supreme joy for me to have been so completely accepted by these people. Though I am different, and stealing one of their native sons, they look at me as good luck. "Baaju" (sister-in-law), they call, and urge me to drink more. A child plops herself in my lap, giggles and grabs for my chang.

Even though some exterior changes have occurred, such as dress, radios, dishes, and so forth, it does not appear that the culture of the Sherpa people has changed dramatically. There will be small changes as time goes on; eventually the changes will accumulate, and the Sherpas will not be who they once were. However, this can be said for any culture. I can see no realistic way that change can be stopped. Everyone desires a successful life, and today, that is synonymous with Western society. Hopefully, the Sherpas will maintain many of the ideas and traditions that make them a distinctive people in Nepal. One thing will continue to remain constant—for anyone who knows anything about mountain climbing, the term that will always spring to mind will be *Sherpa.*

Glossary

I have noted where the word is Sherpa or Nepalese; if not noted, it is either interchangeable between Sherpa and Nepalese or a Western word.

aaune—Nepalese word for come
angi—Sherpa word for Sherpa women's long gowns
arak—Sherpa word for clear alcohol

baaju—Nepalese word for sister-in-law
bechnu—Nepalese word for sell
bhaat—Nepalese word for cooked rice
Bhote Kosi—Bhote is Tibetan for Tibet and Kosi is Nepalese for River
Bhuwa—Sherpa word for Phurba's village; Nepalese word is Shurkey, Surkey, or Surke
Bodnath—Tibetan settlement outside Kathmandu

chang—Sherpa word for native-brewed beer
chappati—Indian word for flat unleavened bread
Chaumrikharka—Nepalese word for a village near Bhuwa/Shurkey that contains the school, it means zum place; Sherpa name is Dhungdae
chepar—Sherpa word for white cloth wrapped around corpse
cheur—Sherpa word for yogurt
chhelma—Nepalese word for a type of Yeti thought of as a forest shaman
chhungyar—Sherpa word for a large water-powered Buddhist prayer wheel
chhuti—Nepalese word for a type of Yeti not harmful to humans
Chomolungama—Tibetan name for Mt. Everest; it means "Goddess Mother of the World"
chorten—Sherpa world for a Buddhist solid monument with domed roof; each contains some kind of relic, such as bones of a famous lama
chya khang—Sherpa word for a flimsy bamboo shelter put up in the fields; where children sleep so they can help protect the ripening crops
circem chetup—Sherpa word for the ceremony to bless the building of a new house
cque—Sherpa word for a soup of flour, salt and water

daal—Nepalese word for lentils
dawa—Sherpa word for moon, month or Monday
Dawa Chiwa—Sherpa word for October/November, their ninth month
Dawa Chuchikpa—Sherpa word for January/February, their twelfth month

Dawa Chungiwa—Sherpa word for December/January, their eleventh
     month
Dawa Chyuchikpa—Sherpa word for November/December, their tenth
     month
Dawa Dyunwa—Sherpa word for August/September, their seventh
     month
Dawa Gyepa—Sherpa word for September/October, their eighth month
Dawa Ngawa—Sherpa word for June/July, their fifth month
Dawa Ngiwa—Sherpa word for March/April, their second month
Dawa Siwa—Sherpa word for May/June, their fourth month
Dawa Sumbu—Sherpa word for April/May, their third month
Dawa Thangpo—Sherpa word for February/March, their first month
Dawa Thukpa—Sherpa word for July/August, their sixth month
Dhadur—Tibetan word for book containing calendar/horoscope
Dharmasol—Tibetan and Sherpa word for temple in Solu area
Dhungdae—Sherpa word for neighboring village that contains school;
     Nepalese word is Chaumrikharka meaning zum place
Dudh Kosi—Nepalese words for Milk River
dumbba—Sherpa words for red clay and water mixture to be placed on
     outside of house's stone walls
Dumje—Sherpa word for general celebration for blessing of village
dupda—Tibetan word for lama who performs rituals
dzopkyo—Sherpa word for the male animal resulting from the mating
     of a male yak and a cow

galu—Sherpa word for large bamboo trays
gengu—Sherpa word for the marriage ceremony
gompa—Nepalese word for temple or monastery
gonda—Sherpa word for temple or monastery
goral—Nepalese word for small wild goat
gurmu—Sherpa word for small bamboo tray
gyipchung—Sherpa word for fox, wolves and jackels
gyou—Sherpa word for rice giving at death ceremony

Himalaya—Home of Snow
ho—Nepalese word for is
hraka—Sherpa word for monkeys with white heads and tails
hrendi—Sherpa word for stiff-backed spirit

Jiri—town in the Solu District at the eastern end of the road
Jorsale—Nepalese word for a village in the Khumbu; Sherpa word is
     Thumbug

kami—Sherpa word for blacksmith
kani—Sherpa word for village entry gate
key—Nepalese word for what
kez zongee—Sherpa word for best type of dog
khangba sam—Sherpa word for a long one-story house
khangba tyangang—Sherpa word for two-story house
khata—Sherpa word for white ceremonial cloth

kheen—Sherpa word for loans
Khumbu—Nepalese word for high place; the northern part of the
    Mount Everest valley
Khumjung—Nepalese word for village in Khumbu
kina—Nepalese word for why
knock—Sherpa word for female yak
kukuri—Nepalese word for traditional, slightly curved knife
kyetee—Sherpa word for woman's silver belt buckle

la—Sherpa word for a mountain pass
lama—Tibetan and Sherpa word for priest
lammergeyer—golden vulture
lha—Sherpa word for small hopping animal
Lhakpa—Sherpa word for Wednesday
lhawa minung—Sherpa word for shaman
Losar—Sherpa word for New Year
Lukla—Nepalese word for airport town of Khumbu; means sheep
Lupsang—Sherpa word for personal ceremony for blessing a house

mani—Sherpa word for carved stone
Mani-Rimdu—Sherpa word for Buddhist dance festival
matril—Sherpa word for Sherpa woman's apron
martze—Sherpa word for chilis
Mingma—Sherpa word for Tuesday
miti—Nepalese word for type of Yeti that are very harmful to people
moomoo—Sherpa word for dumpling with meat and spices inside
moraine—stones pushed before a glacier
Mushay—Nepalese word for neighboring village to Bhuwa/Shurkey;
    Sherpa word for village is Nakbug

Nakbug—Sherpa word for neighboring village to Bhuwa/Shurkey;
    Nepalese word is Mushay
Namaste—Nepalese word for greeting, said with hands together in
    prayer
Namche Bazaar—Nepalese word for main village of Khumbu; Sherpa
    word is Nauche
Naphur—Sherpa word for death ceremony
ngalok—Sherpa word for reciprocal work
nigalya ponya—Nepalese word and scientific name for red panda
Nima—Sherpa word for Sunday
nying-ma-pa—subsect of Buddhism that the Sherpas practice
nyuthi—Sherpa word for benches

Om Mani Padme Hum—Sherpa words that are the beginning of the
    main Buddhist prayer; meaning "The Jewel is in the Lotus"

pangboche—Nepalese word for village in Khumbu
Pasang—Sherpa word for Friday
paunch pokari—Nepalese word for five lakes
pem—Sherpa word for spirit of light that roams at night
Pemba—Sherpa word for Saturday

pembu—Sherpa word for tax collectors
Pharak—Sherpa word for the valley that connects the Solu and
    Khumbu areas
Phortse—Nepalese word for village in Khumbu
Phurba—Sherpa word for Thursday
phurdon puntza—Sherpa word for village headman
polyandry—two or more men marrying one woman
polygyny—two or more women marrying one man
puck—Sherpa word for whitewash

rakshi—Nepalese word for clear alcohol
remmun—Sherpa word for weasel
riki—Sherpa word for potato
rikuma—Sherpa word for very thin, long potato
ril ducsan—Sherpa word for mashed potatoes made using potatoes,
    water and flour
rkik—Sherpa word for red monkey
rongpishur—Sherpa word for porcupine

sabkhang—Sherpa word for a small (short) one-story house
Sagarmatha—Nepalese name for Mount Everest
sal—soft wood
salika—Sherpa word for kinship group to which Phurba belongs
Salleri—Nepalese word for district capital of Solu Khumbu located in
    the Solu
sanchung—Sherpa word for beer made from corn or millet
sang-ngag—the secret formulas of Buddhism
sardar—head guide
seta—Tibetan word for lama who teaches
shay—Sherpa word for drink (verb)
shaytu—Sherpa word for lamas reading scriptures at death ceremony
shayzum—Sherpa word for death ceremony to make sure that the
    dead person does not come back and haunt the house
sherpa—Sherpa word for guide
shommar—Sherpa word for fermented sour milk
shommar sondu—Sherpa words for soup made with shommar, water,
    chilis and salt
shoshem—Sherpa word for scum from the inside of a milk bucket
Shurkey—Nepalese word for Phurba's village, also spelled Surkey or
    Surke; Sherpa word is Bhuwa
Shurkey Khola—Nepalese words for river running through Phurba's
    village
Sipakhorlo—Sherpa word for wheel of life
Solu—Nepalese word meaning lowlands; the area leading up to the
    Pharak (Everest) valley
Sonam—Sherpa word for merit
syamjar—Sherpa word for traditional woman's blouse

tahr—Nepalese word for a large brown mountain goat
tatok—spirits of the dark

te—Sherpa word for animal

Tenjyuk—Sherpa word for last heavy rainfall ending the monsoon in September

Thangboche—leading Buddhist monastery in Khumbu

thangkas—Tibetan word for wheel of life

Thumbug—Sherpa word for village in Khumbu; Nepalese word is Jorsale

thukpa—Sherpa word for noodle-based stew

tho—Sherpa word for tuber

Tibetan tea—tea, salt, milk and butter churned together

tole—Sherpa word for male animal resulting from mating of a zum and a regular bull

tolmu—Sherpa word for a female animal resulting from mating of a zum and a regular bull

tongba—Sherpa word for alcoholic drink brewed from millet

torma—Sherpa word for sacrificial cakes

trek—hike

Tsah—Sherpa word for thanksgiving ceremony

tsah lhawa—Sherpa words for people who give torma during tsah ceremony

tsampa—Sherpa word for roasted barley flour mixed with water to form a dough

tsaou—Sherpa word for bamboo-plaited baskets

ungma—Sherpa word for a shed made from bamboo with roof and low half-walls

yak—Sherpa word for high-altitude bull with long, thick hair

yang—Sherpa word for good luck

ye—Sherpa word for rock

yerjyuk—Sherpa word for heavy monsoon rains of August

Yeti—Sherpa word for abominable snowman

yo—Nepalese word for this

yungnay—Sherpa word for fall ceremony for gaining merit

zik—Sherpa word for snow leopard

zum—Sherpa word for female animal resulting from mating a male yak and a cow

Sherpa Vocabulary

- ► all vowels are sounded the same as in English. *aa* is a long, low, unsounded *a* such as in *father*
- ► *kh, gh, ch, jh, Th, Dh, ph, bh,* are all aspirated
- ► *ng* such as in *finger*
- ► *chh*—voiceless aspirated counterpart of *ch.* There is no equivalent in English.
- ► *t, d, k*—soft sound
- ► *T, D, K*—hard sound
- ► *dh, th*—non-aspirated, soft sound
- ► *r*—is a rolled sound

---

aama—mother
aani—father's sister
achhu—older brother
angi—woman's long gown
ani—nun
arak—alcoholic drink
aring—today
au—father's brother
azhzhe—sister

bald kopi—cabbage
baraa kungba—apartment
bin—give
bung knee—very

cha—bird, chicken
chagung kaneway—bathroom
chang—beer
charwau—rain
chaymanda—egg
cheese —cheese
chetamba—ten
cheur—yogurt
chha—tea

chhungyar—water-powered
   prayer wheel
chick—one
chickrung—alone
chini—sugar
Chomolungama—Mount Everest
chormung—expensive
chorten—Buddhist monument
chu—water
chumba lasung—thirsty
chungma—cow
chya khang—bamboo shelters in
   fields
circem chetup—ceremony for
   good luck in building a house
conshe—youngest sister
cque—flour and salt drink

da—enemy
dalza—friend
daotzung—full
dawa—month, moon, Monday
Dawa Chiwa—October/November,
   ninth month

127

Dawa Chuchikpa—
  January/February, twelfth
  month
Dawa Chungiwa—
  December/January, eleventh
  month
Dawa Chyuchikpa—
  November/December, tenth
  month
Dawa Dyunwa—
  August/September, seventh
  month
Dawa Gyepa—September/October,
  eighth month
Dawa Ngawa—June/July, fifth
  month
Dawa Ngiwa—March/April, second
  month
Dawn Siwa—May/June, fourth
  month
Dawa Sumbu—April/May, third
  month
Dawa Thangpo—February/March,
  first month
Dawa Thukpa—July/August,
  sixth month
dawsa—help
day—sit
de—this
dha—rice
dhadur—calendar/horoscope
digpa—sin
din—seven
dorje—sceptre
dumbba—red clay and water,
  mixed
dung—yesterday
dupda—lama who performs
  rituals
dzopkyo—male produced by
  mating male yak and cow

eyeple—apple

gaa—eight
gairbu—big
galatzung—happy
galu—large bamboo tray
garmu—small bamboo tray

gengu—marriage ceremony
ghiu—go
gho—door
ghoo—wait
gna—five
gomung—evening gonda—temple,
  monastery
goo—nine
gopa—garlic
gyiupchung—fox, wolf, jackel
gyou—death ceremony, rice
  giving

hako sung—understand
hlo lasun—hungry
hlow—look
hraka—monkey with white head
  and tail
hrendi—stiff-backed spirit

kaa—snow
kami—blacksmith
kamu—cheap
kani—village entrance gate
kayga—gift
keraa—banana
kermu—white
kez zongbee—best dog
khan—steep
khangba—house
khangba sam—large (long) one-
  story house
khangba tyangang—two-story
  house
kharmo—sweets
khata—white religious scarf
kheen—loans
khurrung—you
kimbok—spoon
knee—two
knelock—sleep
knock—high-altitude, shaggy-
  haired, female cow
knockpu—black
koolee—slow
kuma—long, thin white potato
kung—what
kya—husband
kyetee—silver buckle

kyiuyp—breakfast

la—mountain pass
lakpa—some more
lemmu—good
lha—hopping animal
Lhakpa—Wednesday
lhawa minung—shaman
lo—year
Losar—New Year
lupsang—general house blessing

main bhatti—candles
mani—prayer wheels and walls
    with prayers carved into them
Mani-Rimdu—Buddhist dance
    festival
manja—clothes
mar—butter
martung—dizzy
martze—chili
matril—apron
may—fire
maylow—bed
me—man
mellow—not good
mendaugh—flower
mik—eye
milam—dream
min—name
Mingma—Tuesday
moomoo—dumpling
mukpa—cloudy
mung—don't come

naaso—rest, stop
Naphur—cremation ceremony
nating—forest
nawp—buy
nearmu—afternoon
ngalok—reciprocal work
Nima—Sunday, sun
nup—younger brother
nyuthi—benches

ohma—milk
Om Mani Padme Hum—main
    Buddhist prayer beginning;
    "The Jewel is in the Lotus"

papa—father

Pasang—Friday
pay—flour
paza—children
pear retze—beans
pem—spirits of light
Pemba—Saturday
permin—wife
phum—daughter
Phurba—Thursday
phurree—cucumber
poojung—son
puck—whitewash
pulgope—cauliflower
pumpeasa—woman

ree—ridge
remmun—weasel
riki—potato
ril ducsan—mashed potatoes
rkik—red monkey
rong pishur—porcupine

sa—earth
sabkhang—small (short) one-story
    house
sabun—soap
sala—tomorrow
sama—food
sanchung—beer
sang ngag—secret formulas in
    Buddhism
seta—lama who teaches
sha—meat
shay—drink (verb)
Shay Tu—death ceremony;
    scripture reading
Shayzum—death ceremony; ghost
    prevention
she—four
shing—wood
shirrak—blanket
shock—come
shommar—sour, fermented milk
shoshem—scum from milk bucket
shoulke nock—diarrhea
Sipakhorlo—wheel of life
somatzo—cook something
sonam—merit
sondu—soup

sook gaino—pain
subje—vegetables
sum—three
syamjar—traditional woman's
    blouse
szo—eat

tahr—mountain goat
tangga—cold
tayla—straight
te—animal
tekgai geno—alright
tenjyuk—last large rain of
    monsoon in September
thaa—wheat
thangkas—wheel of life
thing knough—follow
tickbey—a little
tillu—bell
tole—male produced by mating
    zum and bull
tolma—female produced by
    mating zum and bull
tool la—descend, down
tongba—millet alcoholic drink
torma—sacrificial cakes
toup—six
Tsah—thanksgiving ceremony
tsampa—roasted barley flour
tsaou—breakfast
tsungbe tangga—river bank
tuck tuk—all
tungbu mindu—sick
tungga—money
tung gho—drink

tza—salt
tzekda—match
tzende—hot
tzol mung—easy
tzotup—boiled
tzow—cost
tzungbu—river
tzungu—sell

unga—baby
ungma—bamboo

woltuk—wind
woodshshe—no

yak—high-altitude bull
yang—luck
yanglung—and
yanlung—again
yawwa—right
ye—rock
yemba—left
yerjyuk—heavy monsoon rains of
    August
yin—yes
yungnay—personal merit
    ceremony

za—day
zeemu—beautiful
zik—snow leopard
zockboo—corn
zu—body
zum—female produced by mating
    male yak and cow

English to Nepalese Vocabulary

- ► all vowels are sounded the same as in English. *aa* is a long, low, unsounded *a* such as in *father*
- ► *kh, gh, ch, jh, Th, Dh, ph, bh,* are all aspirated
- ► *ng* such as in *finger*
- ► *chh*—voiceless aspirated counterpart of *ch*. There is no equivalent in English.
- ► *t, d, k*—soft sound
- ► *T, D, K*—hard sound
- ► *dh, th*—non-aspirated, soft sound
- ► *r*—is a rolled sound

(to be) able to—saknu
about—andaaji, baaremaa jati
above—maathi
ache—dukhnu
across—paari
Adam's apple—rudra ghanti
afraid—dar laagnu
after that—tyaspachhi
afternoon—diuso
again—pheri
ago—aghi
agriculture—krishi
airplane—hawaai jahaajmaa
all—sabai
all right—thik hunu
all the time—kahile pani
almost—jhanDai
alone—saraasar
along—saraasar
alphabet—ahshar

also—pani
altogether—jamma
always—sadhai, kahile pani
am—hu
among—maddhye
and—ra
and how about—ni
and then—ani
angry—risaaunu
ankle—goli gaathaa
answer—jawaaph
ant—Kamilaa
any—Kehi
anybody—Kohi
anything—aru, kepani, kun pani
apartment—Deraa
apple—syaau
apricot—Khurpaari
are—laagyo, chhan, hun
area—chhetra

argument—bibaad
arm—waripari
around here—yahaa
(to) arrive—pugnu
arrow—tir
article—lehh
as far as—samma
ash tray—Kharaani daari
(to) ask for—maagnu
asparagus—Kurilo
ass—chak
(to) assist—maddat garnu
at—maa
attempt—kosis garnu
available—paainchha
(on the) average—saalaa khaalaa
awake—jaagnu
away from—TaaDhaa
awhile—ekchhin
axe—bancharo

baby—bachchaa
back—pachare, piThyu
backbone—DhaaD
ballpoint pen—Dat pen
bamboo—baas
banana—Keraa
bank (river)—kinaar
barber—naau, hajaam
bark (dog)—bhuKnu
bark (tree)—baKraa
barley—jau
basket (porters)—Doko tokari
(to) bathe—nuhaaunu
bathroom—sauchaalaya
bat—chamero
beach, bank—Kinaar
beans—simi
beard—daarhi
(to) beat (eggs)—pheTnu
because—kina bhane
beautiful—sandar
bed—raati
bed (to make)—ochhyaan
    milaaunu
beer—bijaar
beets—chuKandar

behind—pachhaa Di
belch—Dakaarnu
beloved—premiKaa
below—muni
bend (a stick)—bangyaauna
bend over—jhuKnu
beside—chheumaa
(the) best—sabbhandaa
between—bichmaa, muni,
    maddhye
bicycle—saaikal
bind—baadhnu
bird—charaa
bite (food)—Toknu
bitter—tito
black—Kalo
blacksmith—Kaami
blanket—Kambal
bleed—ragat aaunu
blood—Khun, ragat
blow (a fire)—phuKnu
blow (wind)—haawaa, bahanu
blue—nilo
boasting—dhaak
boat—Dungaa
body hair—rau
boiled—usineko, umeleko
bone—haaD
book—Kitaab
boots—suebas
bore (a hole)—pwaal paarnu
bored—dikkalagnu
both—Dubai
bottle—sisi
bottom—tallo
boy—Ketaa
branch—haagaa
bread—roti
break—phuTnu
break (a rope)—chuDaaunu
breakfast—bihaanakoKhaana
breast—chhaati
breathe —saas phernu
bride—dulahi
bridegroom—dulaahaa
bring—lyaaunu
bring along—lagiraakhnu

(to) bring for someone—lyaaidinu
bridge, good—pul
bridge, bad—saaghu
bright—chahakilo
broker—dalaal
brother, older—daaju, daai
brother, younger—bhaai
brother's daughter—bhatiji
brother's son—bhatijaa
  older brother's wife—bhaauju
  younger brother's wife—buhaari
brown—khairo
Buddhist monument—chorten
Buddhist teacher—rinposhay
buffalo—raango
build (a house)—banaaunu
building—bhawan
bully—DaaTnu
bundle—poKaa
burn—balnu
bury—gaaDnu
bush—jhaaDi
businessman—byaapaari
but—tara
butcher—maarnu, kasaai, bagare
butter—ghiu, makhan
butterfly—putali
buy—Kinnos
by—dwaaraa

cabbage—ban daa kopi
call—DaaKnu
call out—bolaaunu
candles—mainbatti
capital—raajdhaani
cards—taas
carpenter—sikarmi
carpet—galaichha
carrots—gaajar
carry—boknu
carry for someone—lagi dinu
(in that) case—usobhae
cashews—kaaju
caste—jaat
catch—samaatnu
cauliflower—Kaauli
certain—Thegaan
certainly—abasya

chair—Kursi, mech
change (money)—saaTi dinu
charcoal—koilaa
cheap—sasto
cheek—gala
cheese—chij
chest —chaati
chew (food)—chapaaunu
chicken—KuKhura
chili—Khursaani
chin—chiuDo
China—Chin
chives—chhyaapi
choose—rojnu
cigarette—churot
cigarette, one—khilli
city—shahar
clean—saphaa
clerk—kaarindaa
clearly—chharlangai
clever—baaTo
climb—charnay, chaDhnu
(to) close—banda garnu
close kin—saakhhai
clothes—lugaa
cloth—KapaDaa
cloth merchant—Kapadaa Pasale
cloudy—baakal laagyo
coal—gol
cobbler—saarki
coconut—nariwal
cold—jaado
cold water—chiso pani
(have a) cold—rughaa laagyo
cold drink (sweet)—sarbat
color—rang
colorful—rangi changi
comb—Kaaiyo
comb (hair)—Kornu
come—aaunos
contractor—bhaanse
consult with the doctor—
    daakTarlaai dekhaaunu
(don't) come—na aau
(don't) cook—pakaaunos
(don't) copy—nahkal
corn—makai

corner—Kunaa
cost—parchha, mol
(does not) cost—pardaina
cotton cloth—sutiKapalDaa
cough—KhoKnu
count—gannu
country—desh
courtyard—aagan, chok
cover—DhaaKnu
cow—gaai
crack—pwaal, chiraa
crooked—baango
crow (bird)—Kaa
crow (rooster)—baasnu
crowd—bhiD
crush—nichornu
cry (weep)—runu
cucumber—Kaakro
cup and saucers—pyaalaa ra
    rikaabi
cured—nikohunu
curtain—pardaa
cut (rope)—KaaTnu
cut (food)—Tukraa paarnu
cut through—chhinnu

dance—naachnu
dark—adhyaaro
date, Nepali—gate
date, English—taariKh
date (fruit)—chhohoraa
daughter—Kaanchhi chhori
daughter's husband—juwaai
day—din, baar
day after tomorrow—parsi
day before yesterday—asti
daylong—dinbhari
daytime—diuso
descend—jharnu
desire—rahar
destroy—bigaarnu
diarrhea—dishaa laagnu
die—marnu
different—pharak
difficult—mushkil, gaarho
dig (hole)—Khannu
dig up—Khannu

(in what) direction—Kataatira
dirty—phohor
discipline—anushaashan
discover—pattaa lagaaunu
dissolve—galnu
District Center—Sadar Mukaam
divide—bhaag lagaaunu
dizzy—ringaTaa
do—garnos
don't come—na aau
don't know—thaa chaina
don't need—chaain daina
do not put—raakhnos
don't want—man laagdaina
do you like—man parchha
do you want—man laagchha
dog—Khur
door—DhoKaa
down—tala
downhill—oraalo
drag —Taannu
drainage—Dhal
draw (sketch)—chitra Khichhnu
drink—Khannu peanus
(to) drive—chalaaunu
drop—Khasaainu
drum—tabla
drunk—raksi laagnu
dry field—baari
dry out—sukaaunu, suknu
(to) dust—saphaa garnu
dust—dhulo

early—chhiTo
earn—Kamaaunu
ear—Kaan
early morning—sabare
easily—sajilai
east—purba
easy—sajilo
eat—Khaanu
(I have) eaten—Khaaeho chhu
(to) eat a meal (polite)—bhaansaa
    garnu
editor—sam paadak
education—sikchhya
egg—phul

elbow—kuhino
empty—Khaali paarnu
enough—pugnu
envelope—Khaam
equal—baraabar
et cetera—aadi
evening—beluka
every—harek
examine—jaachnu
exceedingly—nikaai
excuse me—hajur
expensive—mahango
extinguish—nibhaaunu
extremely—asaadhyai, audhi
eye—aKaa

face—mukh
factory—KaarKhaanaa
fall—Khasnu, paryo
fall (rain)—paani parnu
family—pariwaar
famous—prasiddha
far from—Taakhaa
farm—Ketbaari, bagaichaa
farmer—Kisaar
farming—Krishi
fast—chhiTo
fat—moTo, boso
father—baabu, baa
father-in-law—sasuraa
father-in-law's house—sasuraali
father's elder brother—Thulobaa
father's elder brother's
    wife—Thuli
father's younger brother—Kaakaa
father's younger brother's
    wife—Kaaki
father's sister—phupa
father's sister's
    husband—phupaaju
fatigue—thaKaai
faucet—dhaaro
fear—Dar
feast —bhoj
feather—pwaakh
feel—chhunu
fence—baar

festival—chaaD
fetch—lyaaunu
fever—jwaro
few—thorai
field—Khetbaari
fight—laDaai, jhagaDaa garnu
fill (bottle)—bharnu
find—pattaa lagaaunu
finger—aulaa
fingernail—nang
(to be) finished—siddhinu
(to take from) fire—Taarnu
fire—aago
firefly—junkiri
firewood—daauraa
first—pahilo
fish—maachhaa
fishnet—jaal
flame—jwaalaa
flour—piThu, tsampa
flea—upiyaa
flood—baaDhi
floor—bhui
flow—bagnu
flower—phul
flute—baasuri
(to) fly—uDnu
fly (insect)—jhingaa
fog—Kuiro
fold (cloth)—paTyaaunu
follow—maannu
food—Khaana
food for one meal—chaak
foot—pinetalu, Khutto (and leg)
(on) foot—hiDera
foot long—phiT
for—waTaa, Kilaagi
for this—yasko
forehead—nidhaar
foreigner—badashi
forest—ban
fork —KaaTaa
forty—chaalis
found—paainchha
free time—phursad
Friday—sukrabaar
friend—saathi

friendly—milansaar
frog—bhyaagutaa
(in) front of—agaaDi
from—baaTaa
fruits—phalphul
fry—bhuTnu
frying pan—taawaa
full—bhari
(I'm) full—pugyo
fun—majaa

garbage—phohor
garden—bagaichha
gardener—maali
garlic—lasun
get—paaunu
gift—daan
girl—KeTi
give—dinos
glass—gilass
go—jaau
goat—Kasi
god—iswar
going—janne
goldsmith—sunaar
good—raamro, bas, asal
  much good—raamro sahrai
  not good—na raamro
  very good—dherai raamro
gossip—gaph garnu
government—sarKaari
government official—sarkaari
granddaughter—naatini
grandfather—baaje
grandmother—bajai
grandson—naati
grape—angur
grapefruit—bhogate
grass—ghaas
grasshopper—phaTengraa
green—hariyo
ground—jamin
ground over—chulho
group—bathaan

habit—baani
hair—case, Kapaal

half—aaddhaa
half past—saaDhe
half rupee—mohar
hand—haat
happy—Khushi
hard—KaDaa, saarho
hat—topi
have—bhaeko
he—usle
head—Taauko
(to be) heard—suninu
heart—dil
heat—tap
heel—Kurkuchchha
hello—Namaste
help—madat
here—yahaa
hey you (feminine)—e daai
hiccup—hikka aaunu
(to) hide—luknu
highway—raajmaarga
hill—DaaDaa
his—wahaako, usko
His Majesty the King—Sir Paach
    Mahaaraajaad Hiraaj
history—itihaasnu, Thok
hit—haannu, piTnu, Thok
hold—samaatnu
hold out—thaap
hole—pwaal
holiday—bidaa, chhuTTi
hollow—KhoKro
holy place—tirthasthaan
home—ghar
honey—maha
hook (fish)—balchhi
horse—ghoDaa
hot—taato, garmi
hour—ghantaa
house rent—bhaaDaa baahaal,
    Kiraayaa
how—Kasto, Kati, Kasari
(and) how about—ni
how much—Kattiho
hundred—saya
hundred rupee note—nambari
hungry—bhok laagyo

husband—logne, srimaan
husband's eldest
        brother—jeThaana
husband's eldest brother's
        wife—jeThaani
husband's youngest
        brother—dewar
husband's youngest brother's
        wife—deuraani
husband's eldest sister—aamaaju
husband's youngest sister—nanda
hymn—bhajan

I—ma
idea—bichaar
in/inside—bhitra
inn—bhaTTi
insane—baula
in—maa
intensively—dhumdhaam
is—ho, chaa, hunchha
it's—yasko
itch—chilaaunu

jaw—bangaaro
job—Kaam
jobless—baKaar
join—gornu, missinu, joDnu
juice—ras
jump—uphranu
just like that—ustai

kerosene—mattitel
kettle—Kitli chiyaadaari
kick—laat haannu
(to) kill—maarnu
kin—naatedaar
kind—kisim
kinship—naataa
knee—ghuDaa
knife—chaKKu
knot—gaaTho
(I don't) know—Kunni
know—jaannu
(to) know—thaahaa hunu chinnu
(to not) know—thaahaa chhaina
knowledge—gyaan

laborer—jyaami

ladder—bharyaang
lake—tal
lamp—batti
landlord—gharpati
language—bhaasaa
large—Thulo
last—gaeko
last year—phor (saal)
latch—chheskini, chukul
late—Dhilo, abelaa
laugh—haasnu
lawyer—wakil
lazy—alchhi
lead—lagnu
leaf—paat
leaf vegetable—saag, paat
(to) learn—siknu
(to) leave—chhoDi dinu
leave behind—pachaaDi
leech—jukaa
left—baayaa
left over (telling time)—baaki
leg—Koota
leisure—phursad
lemon—Kaagati
lentils— daal
less—Kam
letter—chiTTi, patra
lid—birko
lie—jhuTho, jhut, DhaaTnu
lie down—palTanu
lift up—uThaaunu
light—batti
light (in color)—ujyaalo
(to) light—baalnu
(to) turn off the light—nibhaaunu
like—man parnu, jasto
like that—jattiKai
(not) like—man pardaina
lima bean—Thulo simit
line (mark)—chino
listen—sunnos
(a) little—ali ali
live—basnu
living room—baiThak KooThaa
load—bhaari
lodging—baas

long—laamo
look—hernos
(to) look for—Khojnu
loose—KhuKulo
lose—haraaunu
loud (call)—Thulo
louse—jumraa
lover—premi
luke warm—mantaato
lucky—baagay man

(be) made—bannu, baneko
magician—jaadugar
make—bannle, banaaunu
man, old—bhDho
man, young—tanderi
mango—aap
map—naksaa
mark—Daam, chino, lagaaunu
market—bajaar
marriage—bihaa
mason—Dakarmi
mat—gundri
match—salaai
maybe—holaa
(to) measure—naapnu
meat—maasu
  buffalo—raango
  chicken—KuKhura
  beef—gaai
  goat—Kasi
medicine—ausadhi
(to) meet—bheTnu
melt—paglanu
mend—bannaaunu
merriment—rang
middle—bichmaa
milk—dudh
mine—mero
  plural—meraa
mirror—ainaa
mischievous—badmaas
miss (a target)—nalaagnu
(to) mix—nisaaunu
moment—chhin
Monday—sombaar
money—paisaa
month—mahina

moon—chandramaa, jun
more—aru, jhan, baDhi
morning—bihaara
morning meal—bihaaeKo
  Khaanaa
mosquito—laamKhuTTe
(the) most—sabbhandaa
mostly—dherai jaso
mother—aamaa
mother-in-law—saasu
mother's brother—maamaa
mother's brother's wife—maaiju
mother's sister—saanima
mother's sister's
  husband—saanabaa
mother's father—baaje
mother's mother—bajai
mountains—himal, pahaaD
mouse—musaa
mouth—mukh
much—bhayo
mud—hilo
museum—sangrahaalaya
mushroom—chyaau
must—parchha
my—mero

nail (finger or toe)—nang
name—naam
narrow—saaguro
navel—naaiTo
near—najik, nira
nearby—najiKai
neck—ghaaTi
necklace—haar, maalaa
(is) needed—chaainchaa
needle—siyo
nest—guD
never—Kahile pani
new—nayaa
newspaper—patriKaa
nice—sundar
night—raati
nightmare—aiThan
no—a-ha, chhaina
no it isn't—hoina
no I didn't—aaina

noisy children—chakchake
noodles—chaau chaau
north—uttar
nose—naak
(do) not—na
not available—paaindaina
not like—man pardaina
notebook—Kopi
now—ahile, aba
numbers:

1—ek
2—dui
3—teen
4—char
5—paach
6—chaa
7—saat
8—aTT
9—nau
10—das
11—egara
12—bharra
13—terha
14—chaudha
15—pandhara
16—sorha
17—satra
18—aThaara
19—unnais, unis
20—bis
21—akkaais
22—baais
23—tais
24—chaubis
25—pachchis
26—chhabbis
27—sattaais
28—aThThaais
29—unantis, untis
30—tis
31—ektis
32—battis
33—tattis
34—thautis
35—paitis
36—chhattis
37—saitis

38—aThThis
39—unanchaalis
40—chaalis
41—akchaalis
42—bayaalis
43—trichaalis
44—chawaalis
45—paltaalis
46—chayaalis
47—satchaalis
48—aThchaalis
49—unanchaas
50—pachaas
51—akaaunna
52—baaunna
53—tripanna
54—chaunna
55 —pachpanna
56—chhapanna
57—santaunna
58—anThaaunna
59—unansaaThi
60—saaThi
61—aksaThThi
62—baisaThThi
63—trisaThThi
64—chaasaThThi
65—paisaThThi
66—chhaisaThThi
67—satsaThThi
68—aThsaThThi
69—unansattari
70—sattari
71—akahattar
72—bahattar
73—trihattar
74—chauhattar
75—pachahattar
76—chhahattar
77—satahattar
78—aThahattar
79—unaasi
80—asi
81—akaasi
82—bayaasi
83—triyaasi
84—chauraasi

85—pachaasi
86—chayaasi
87—sattasi
88—aThaasi
89—unaanabbe
90—nabbe
91—edaanabbe
92—bayaanabbe
93—triyaanabbe
94—chauraanabbe
95—panchaanabbe
96—chhayaanabbe
97—santaanabbe
98—anThaanabbe
99—unaansae
100—sae, saya
1,000—hajaar
10,000—das hajaar
100,000—laakh
1,000,000—das laakh

nurse (midwife)—dhaai

o'clock—baje
occupation—peshaa
ocean—mahaasaagar
official (government)—sarkaari
of this—yasko
office—Kaaryaalaya
officer—aphisar, aahiKaari
oil—tel
okay—Thik chha
    polite—hunchha
    very polite—haas
old—puraano
on—maa, maathi
onion—pyaaj
only—maatra
one—ek, chaani
one and a half—DeDh
once—ed paTak
(to) open—ughaarnu, Kholnu
organ (hand)—madal
orphan—anaath
or—Ki
orange (color)—suntala, rang
orchids—sungaabhaa
ornament—gahanaa

other—aru
outside—baahira
ours—haamro
over there—u
own—aaphno

pack—baTTa
paddy—dhaan
pain—dukhnu
paint—rangaaunu
pair—jor
palm—hatKelaa
partnership—saajhaa
pat on back—Dhaap
pay—jyaalaa, talab
peach—aaru
peanuts—badaam
pear—nashpati
peas—Keraau
peel—taachhnu
pen—Kalam
(ball point) pen—Dat pen
pencil—sisaa Kalam
people—janna
percent—pratisat
person—maachee
pick (fruits)—Tipnu
pick up—uThaaunu
piece—bhaag, Tukraa
(a) piece—euTaako
pierce—pwaalpaarnu
pig, tame—sungur
    wild—badel
    improved—bangur
pile up—thupaarnu
pillar—thaam
pillow—takiyaa, siraani
pineapple—bhuiKaTahar
place—Thaau, Thaam
plain—samma
plant—ropnu
plate—thaal
    small—rikaapi
play—Khelne
play (a drum)—bajaau
playing cards—taas
pleasant—ramaailo
(to) please—Klausi paarnu

plum—aarubaKhaDaa
pocket—Kaliti
point—bindu
point at—deKhaaunu
poinsettia—laalupaate
poison—bish
pole—Khaabo
pompously—dhumdhaam
pond—pokhari
population—janasanKhyaa
post—Khaabo
potato—allu
pots and pans—bhaaDaa KuDaa
potter—Kumhaale
pour—Khanyaaunu
(to) prepare—taiyaar garnu
press—thichnu
pretty—sundar
price—daam, mol
probably—holaa
pull—taannu
pumpkin—parsi
punishment—sajaaya
purple—pyaaji
push—dhakelnu
put—raaknos, haalnu
put off—Taarnu
put on (clothes)—lagaaunu

quarter to—paune
quarter past—sawaa
quarter of rupee—sukaa
quickly—chhiTo
quiet (children)—shaanta
quilt—sirak

radish—mulaa
rain—paani parnu, barshaa
(to) raise—paalnu
raisin—Kismis, daakh
rat—musaa
rate—dar
(to) read—paDhnu
(your) rear—chak
rebate—chhut
recognize—chinnu
red—raato
region—chhetra

religion—dharma
relish (hot)—achaar
remaining—baaKi
remove—haTaaunu
rent—bahaal, BhhaDaa
repair—bannaaunu
repeat—dohory aaunu
reply—jawaaph dinu
rest—aaraam garnos
return—pharKanu
rhododendron—garaas
rib—Karang
rice, field—dhaan
    store—chaamal
    cooked—chaat
    pounded—chuiraa
ridge—Dil
right—daayaa
right (correct)—Thik
(all) right—Thik hunu
river—madi
road—baaTo, SaDah
roast—bhuTnu
rope—dori
roof—chhaanaa
room—KoThaa
root—jaraa
rose—gulaab
rotten food—Kuheko, SaDeko
rough (surface)—Kasro
round—golo
rub—dalnu
run—dagurnu
runaway—bhaagnu
rural—gaaule

safety pin—huk, Khip
salary—talab
(for) sale—abasya
salt—nun
same—uhi, ekai
sandals—chapal
Saturday—shanibaar
say—bhannos
scenic—ramaailo
science—bigyaan
scissor—Kaichi
scorpion—bichchhi

scratch (itchy)—Kanyaaunu
scream—chichch yaaunu
(to) scrub—maajhnu, ghoTnu
sea—samudra
search for—Khojnu
be seated—basi raakhnu
secondary school—maadhyamik
    bidyaalaya
secretary—sachib
see—dekhnu
seed—biu
sell—bachnu
send—paThaaunu
servant—noKar
several—anekau
sew—siunu
shade—chhahaari
shadow—chhaayaa
shake—hallaaunu
share—bhaag lagaaunu
sharpen—tikhaarnu
(bed) sheet—tannaa
shelter—ot, baas
shirt—kamij
shit—dishaa
(to) shit—disaa garnu
shiver—Kaannu
shoe—juttaa
shoemaker—saarki
shoot—goli haannu
shop—pasalmaa
(to) shop—Kinmel garnu
shopkeeper—pasale, saahuji
short (long)—chhoto
short (tall)—hocho
shoulder—Kaadh
shoulder bag—jholaa
shout—Karaaunu
show—deKhaaunu
sick—birami
side—chheu
(this) side of river, street—waari
since—aghi, deKhi
sing—git gaaunu
singer—gaayak
silent (person)—nabolne
sir—Kusho

(older) sister—didi
(older) sister's husband—bhinaaju
(younger) sister—bahini
(younger) sister's
    husband—juwaai
(youngest) sister—conshe
sister's daughter—bhaanjis
sister's son—bhaanjaa
sit—basnos
sketch—chitra Khichhnu
skin—chhaalaa
sky—aakaash
sleep—sutnos
sleeping mat—dasnaa
sleepy—nidraa laagyo
(to) slice—Tukraa paarnu
slim—dublo
slow—Dhilo
slowly—bistaari
small—saano
smash (bottle)—phuTaaunu
smell—sughnu
smile—muskuraaunu
smoke—dhuwaa
smooth—chillo
snack—Khaajaa
snake—sarpa
sneeze—haachchiu garnu
sniff—sughnu
snore—ghurnu
snow—hiU
(if) so—uspbhae
soap—saabun
soft—masino
solid—bharilo, Khadilo
soldier—sopaahi
some—Kehi, thorai, Kohi
somebody—Kohi
some more—ajhai
sometimes—Kahile Kaahi
son—chhoraa
son's wife—buhaari
song—git
soot—dhwaaso
sort—Kisim
sour—amilo
south—dakchhin

sow—chharnu
soybeans—bhaTmaas
spreadout—phailaaunu
speak—bolnu
speech—boli
speed—gati
spicy—piro
spider—maakuraa
spinach—saag
spring (of water)—mul
spit—thuKnu
spoon—chamchhaa
spy—jaasus
squeeze—nicharnu
stairs—bharyaang
(be) standing—uThi raakhnu
star—taaraa
state—raajya
steal—chornu
steep—uKaalo
steps—KhuDKilaa, bharyaang
stepmother—sauteni aamaa
(to) stew—suruwa pakaaunu
stick—laTThi
(a long) stick—Taango
stir—pheTnu
stomach—peT
stone—Dhungaa
stone on pass—cairn
(to) stop—roKnu
storekeeper—saahuji
stove (kerosene)—istou
story—talaa
straight—sojho, sidhaa, tersai
strainer—chhaanne
stream—Kholaa
strong—baliyo
student— bidyaarthi
subject—bidyaarthi
subtract—ghaTaau
suck—chusnu
sugar, white—chini
  brown—saKKhar
sugar cane—uKhu
sun—surya, ghaam
Sunday—aitabaar
superiors—Thulaa

swallow—nilnu
sweat—pasinaa aaunu
swell—suninu
sweep (floor)—ba Dhaarnu saphaa
  garnu
sweeper—ba Dhaarne maanchhe
sweet—guliyo
sweets—miThai
sweet potato—sakhar, KhanDa
swim—pauDi Khelnu
system—byawasthaa

tablet—chaKKi
tail—puchchhar
take —linos
taking (eating)—Khaanus
(to) take (carry for someone)—lagi
  dinu
take (there)—lagnu
take off (clothes)—phuKaalnu
talkative—dherai bolne Kuraute
(to) take out—jhiKnu
tall—aglaa
tame—paalnu
tangerine—suntalla
tap—dhaaraa
taro—piDaalu
tasty—miTho
(not) tasty—namiTho
tax—Kar
tea—chiyaa
teacher—sikchhak
tear—chyaatnu
tears—aasu
teeth—daat
tell—bhannu
(to) tell—bataaunu
temple—mandir
thank you—dhanyabad,
    ThyDichhe Thuchhe
that—tyo
that day—tyas din
that much—tyatiKaa
thatch—Khar
then—ta
then if so—usobhae
there (over)—u, tyaahaa
these—yi

they—uniharu
thick (cloth)—baaklo
thigh—tighraa
thin—dublo
thin (cloth)—paatalo
thirty—tis
thirsty—tirkhaa laagnu
this—yo
those—ti
thought—bichaar
thousands—hajaarau
thread—dhaayo
throat—ghaaTi
throw away—phaalnu phhyaaKnu
thumb—buDhi aulaa
Thursday—bihibaar
tie (knot)—baadhnu
time—bajyo, belaa, samaya
tired—thaKaai, nindra
tiger—baagh
tight—Kasieko
Tibetan—tibbati
times—paTak
(at that) time—tyati belaa
to anyone—jaslaaipuni
tobacco leaf—surti
today—aaja
toes—aulaa
toilet—chharpi
tomato—golbhe Daa
tomorrow—bholi
tomorrow morning—bholi
    bhiaana
tongue—jibro
top—maathillo
total—jamma
touch—chhunu
towards—tira
town—shahar
trade—saaTnu
training—taalim
trap (for animals)—Khor dharaap
    paaso
transfer—saruwaa
transportation—yaataayaat
treatment—byabahaar
tree—rukh

trunk—phed
try—Kosis garnu
turn—pharKanu, gum
turn (something over)—palTaaunu
turnip—salgam
Tuesday—mangalbaar
twist (thread)—baTaarnu
twenty-five—pachchis
two and a half—aDhaai
type—Kisim

umbrella—chhaataa
unboiled—umaaleko
uncover—Kholnu
under—tala
understand—bujhnos
unlucky—abhaagi
untie—phuKaaunu
unwrap—Kholnu
(get) up—uThnos
uphill—uKaalo
upper—maathillo
up to—samma
urinate—pisaab garnu
useless—bekaar
useless things—Kaamna laagne
utensils—bhaaDaa KuDaa
usually—dherai jaso

vacant—Knaali
vacation—chhuTTi
valley—besi, upatyaKaa
vegetables—tarKaari
very—dherai, Khub
very (emphatic)—nikaai
very much—assadhyai, ekdam,
    atyanta
very well—Ia
village—gaau
volunteer—sawyam sewak

wages—jyaalaa, talab
waist—Kammar
(to) wait—parKhanu
wake up—uThaaunu, biujhanu
wall—bhittaa, parkhaal
walk—hiDnu
walnut—okhar
wander—ghumnu

want (do you)—man laagnu
warm—nyaano
was—first person—thie
   third person—thiyo
wash (to, clothes)—dhunu
   (to, body)—nuhowna
washed (he)—dueko
washerman—dhobi
waste—Kasingar
watch—ghaDi
water— paani
   drinking—Kaane paani
   boiled—umaaleko paani
   hot—taato paani
   washing—dhune paani
water buffalo—bhaisi
water tap—dhaaro
watermelon—tarbujaa
way—baTo
we—haami
weak—Kachchaa, Kamjor
   nirbaliyo
wear (clothes)—lagaaunu
weather—mausam
weave—bunnu
wedding—bihaa
Wednesday—budhabaar
weed (garden)—goDnu
week—haptaa
well—raamro, inaar
well (you are?)—sanchai chaa
(to be) well—niko huna
well (water)—inaar
went (they)—gae
west—paschim
wet (cloth)—bhijeko
what—Ke
when—Kahile
where—Kahaa
which—Kun
whisper—saauti garnu
white—seto
who—Ko
   plural—KoKo
whole—sabai, jammai
whose—KasKo

why—Kina
wide—pharaakilo
wife—swaasni, srimati
wife's brother—saalaa
wife's sister—saalo
wing—pakheTaa
wild—jangali
window—jhyaal
wind—bataas
wipe—puchhnu
with—saath, sanga
wood—Kaath
wool (for knitting)—un
woolen cloth—uni KapaDaa
woman—swaasni maanchhe,
   aaimai
   old—buDhi
   young—taruni
word—bachan
(to) work hard—mihenat garnu
worship—pujaa
wound—ghaau
wrap around—bern
wraparound gown—chuba
wristwatch—ghaDi
write—lekhna
writer—lekhak

yawn—haai garnu
year—barsa
(last) year—phor
yellow—pahelo
yes—ju, A, Ia
   when addressed—hajur
yes it is—ho
yesterday—hijo
yogurt—dahi
you—tapaai, timi
(and) you?—tapaailaai
you were—thiyau
young girl—ThiTi
your—tapaaiKo

zone—anchal
zoo—chi Diyaa Khaanaa

Bibliography

Abercrombie, Thomas J. 1978. "Ladakh—The Last Shangri-la." *National Geographic* (March).

"AIDS Update." 1991. *Himal Magazine* (July/August), 27.

Bandyopadhyay, Jayanta. 1991. "Mountain Development, Plains' Bias." *Himal Magazine* (March/April), 34.

Bezruchka, Stephen. 1985. *A Guide to Trekking in Nepal.* Seattle: Mountaineers.

Bhatta, Dibya Deo. 1977. *Natural History and Economic Botany of Nepal.* Rev. ed. New Delhi, India: Orient Longman.

Blum, Arlene. 1979. "Triumph and Tragedy on Annapurna." *National Geographic* (March) 1979.

Bohannan, Paul. 1992. *We, The Alien.* Prospect Heights, IL: Waveland Press.

Brower, Barbara. 1992. *The Sherpa of Khumbu: People, Place, Change.* Oxford: Oxford University Press.

Carrier, Jim. 1992. "Gatekeepers of the Himalayas." *National Geographic* (December), 82, 85.

"Carrying Capacity." 1992. *Himal Magazine* (May/June), 45.

"Clean Himalaya." 1991. *Himal Magazine* (July/August), 28.

Dargyay, Eva M. 1977. *The Rise of Esoteric Buddhism.* Delhi, India: Motilal Banarasidas.

"A Dark Winter." 1991. *Himal Magazine* 12 (May/June), 1012–9804.

Discovery World Altas. 1989. Maplewood, NJ: Hammond Incorporated.

Dixit, Kanak Mani. 1991. "Discovering Dharamsala." *Himal Magazine* (March/April), 5–10.

"The Dreck Sack." 1991. *Himal Magazine* (May/June), 21.

Fisher, James F. 1991. "Has Success Spoiled the Sherpa?" *Natural History* (February).

_____. 1990. *Sherpas: Reflections on Change in Himalayan Nepal.* Berkeley: University of California Press.

Gilliard, E. Thomas. 1965. *Living Birds of the World.* New York: Doubleday & Co.

Grzimek's Encyclopedia of Mammals. 1990. New York: McGraw-Hill.

Gyawali, Dipak. 1991. "Troubled Politics of Himalayan Waters." *Himal Magazine* (May/June), 5–10.

Hillary, Sir Edmund. 1984. "Learning About Problems." *Ecology 2000.* London: Michael Joseph.

Joshi, Anup Raj. 1991. "Dharma in Flux." *Himal Magazine* (March/April), 22–23.

Karki, Tika B., and Shrestha, Chij K. 1988. *Basic Course in Spoken Nepali*. Kathmandu, Nepal: Jore Ganesh Press.

Kohli, M. S., and Vergese, B. G. 1962. "The Sherpas." *Himalayan Endeavor*. Bombay: Times of India.

Kothari, Rajni. 1992. "Escaping the Trap of Cultural Diversity," *Himal Magazine* (May/June), 15–16.

Kunwar, Ramesh Raj. 1989. *Fire of Himal*. New Delhi, India: Nirala Publications.

Munro, George Everest. 1991. "The Psychic Pain of New Technology." *Himal Magazine* (July/August), 36.

Ortner, Sherry B. 1989. *High Religion A Cultural and Political History of Sherpa Buddhism*. Princeton: Princeton University Press.

————. 1978. *Sherpas Through their Rituals*. Cambridge: Cambridge University Press.

Pandey, Bikash. 1991. "Let a Thousand Village-Hydros Bloom." *Himal Magazine* (May/June), 18.

Pfaff-Czarnecka, Joanna. 1991. "Bad Business in Bajhang." *Himal Magazine* (May/June), 16–17.

"Return to Everest." 1984. National Geographic Video, part 15645. Stamford, CT: Vestron Inc.

Ridgeway, Rick. 1982. "Park at the Top of the World." *National Geographic* (June).

Sarin, H. C., and Sing, Gyan. 1981. "Mountaineering in the Himalayas." In *The Himalaya Aspects of Change*, edited by J. S. Lall. New Delhi, India: International Centre, 318–38.

Sharma, Prayag Raj. 1992. "How to Tend This Garden?" *Himal Magazine* (May/June), 7–9.

"Sherpas on Top." 1991. *Himal Magazine* (July/August), 27.

Shrestha, D. B., and Singh, C. B. 1987. *Ethnic Groups of Nepal and Their Ways of Living*. Kathmandu, Nepal: Himalayan Booksellers.

Terrell, Paul D., Jr. 1991. "Karnali (Chisapani) in Retrospect." *Himal Magazine* (May/June), 14–15.

The World Almanac. 1990. New York: Pharos Books, 737.

The World Almanac. 1992. New York: Pharos Books, 786.

The World Almanac. 1981. New York: Pharos Books, 561.

The World Atlas. 1989. Maplewood, NJ: Hammond.

Appendix: Kinship Chart

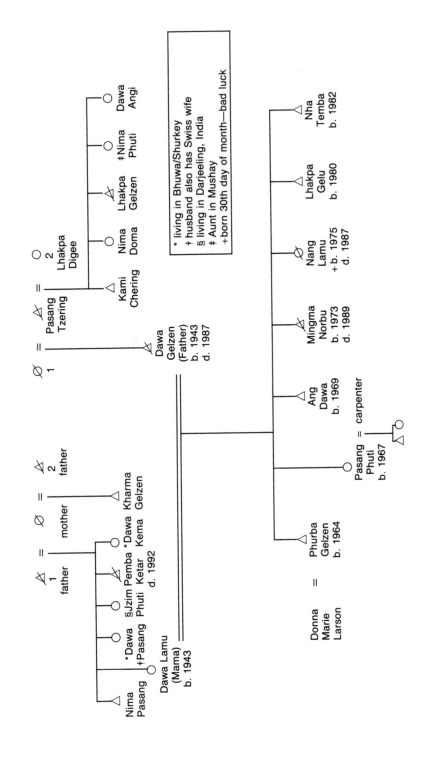

* living in Bhuwa/Shurkey
† husband also has Swiss wife
§ living in Darjeeling, India
‡ Aunt in Mushay
+ born 30th day of month—bad luck

Donna Sherpa has taught high school social studies for many years. She has traveled worldwide, first visiting the Himalayas in 1982. Phurba, her Sherpa husband, was a great influence in this, her first publication about the Sherpa people. Donna and Phurba reside in Camp Hill, Pennsylvania, where they operate Sherpa-tastic Travel (P.O. Box 773, Camp Hill, PA 17011), a hiking company offering guided tours to the Himalayas.

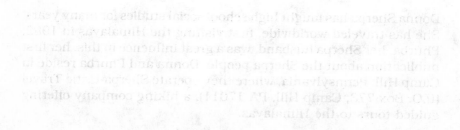

Donna Shepperd is a high school teacher and studies for many years. She has traveled worldwide, first visiting the Himalayas in 1985. Philip J. Shepperd, her husband, was a great influence in this. Her first publication about the Sherpa people, Donna and I Trek to Campbell, Pennsylvania, write, operate Sherpa Treks (P.O. Box 777, Camp Hill, PA 17011), a hiking company offering guided tours to the Himalaya.